Ancient Corinth

Publishers: George A. Christopoulos, John C. Bastias
Translation: Kay Cicellis
Managing Editor: Efi Karpodini
Art Director: Nicos Andricakis
Special Photography: Spyros Tsavdaroglou
Colour separation: Pietro Carlotti

Ancient Corinth

The Museums of Corinth, Isthmia and Sicyon

NICOS PAPAHATZIS

Archaeologist

EKDOTIKE ATHENON S.A.
Athens 2002

ISBN 960-213-143-8

Copyright © 1977
by
EKDOTIKE ATHENON S.A.
1, Vissarionos Street
Athens 106 72, Greece

PRINTED AND BOUND IN GREECE
by
EKDOTIKE HELADOS S.A.
An affiliated company
8, Philadelphias Street, Athens

Contents

Ancient Corinth. The archaic temple.

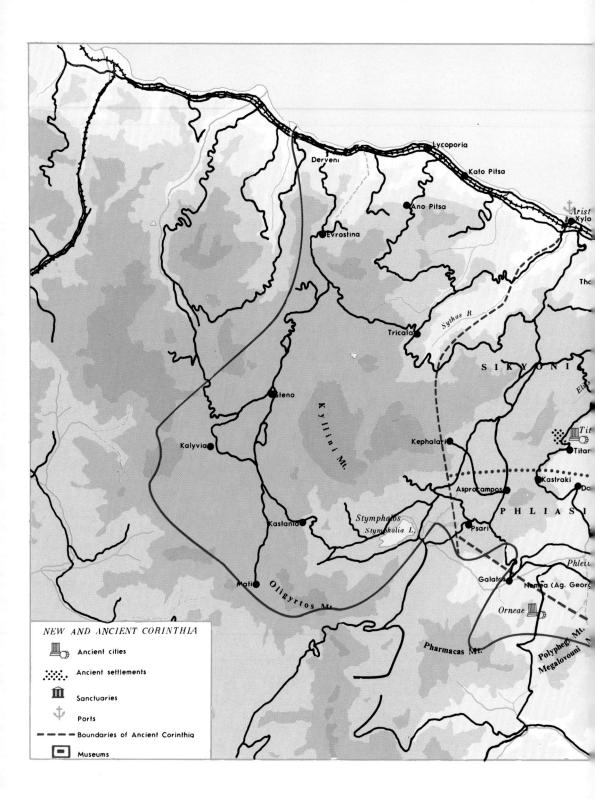

NEW AND ANCIENT CORINTHIA

🏛 Ancient cities

⋮⋮⋮ Ancient settlements

🏛 Sanctuaries

⚓ Ports

– – – Boundaries of Ancient Corinthia

▣ Museums

Lycoporia

Kato Pitsa

Derveni

Ano Pitsa

Arist Xylo

Evrostina

Tho

Sythas R.

Tricala

SIKYONI

Ela

Kyllini Mt.

Steno

Tit

Kephalari

Titan

Kalyvia

Kastraki

Do

Asprocampos

PHLIASI

Kastania

Stymphalos

Stymphalia L.

Psari

Mati

Galates

Nemea (Ag. Georg

Oligyrtos Mt.

Phlei

Orneae

Polypheg Mt.

Pharmacas Mt.

Megalovouni

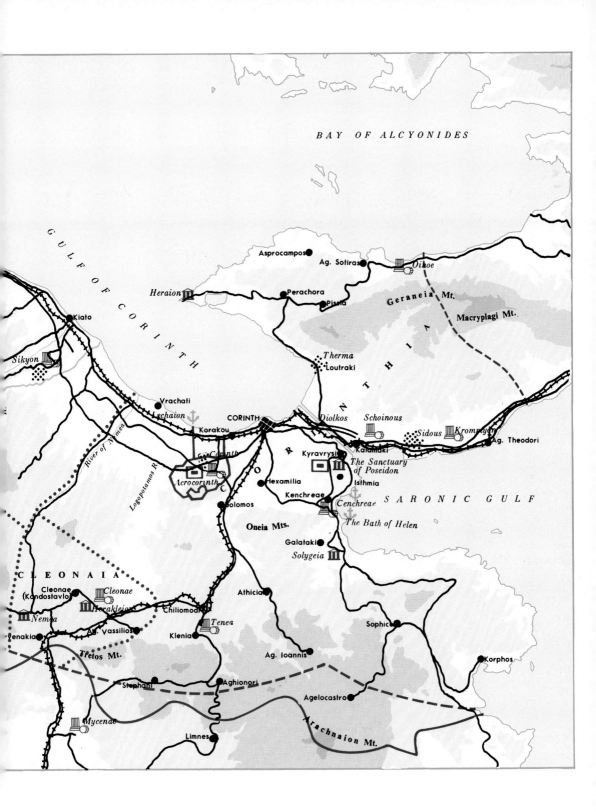

BAY OF ALCYONIDES

GULF OF CORINTH

Asprocampos

Ag. Sotiras

Oinoe

Heraion

Perachora

Pisia

Geraneia Mt.

Macryplagi Mt.

Kiato

Therma

Loutraki

Sikyon

Vrachati

Lychaion

Korakou

CORINTH

Diolkos

Schoinous

Sidous

Kromnyon

Kalamaki

Ag. Theodori

Acrocorinth

Kyravrysi

The Sanctuary
of Poseidon

River of Nemea

Logopotamos R.

Solomos

Hexamilia

Kenchreae

Isthmia

Cenchreae

SARONIC GULF

Oneia Mts.

The Bath of Helen

CLEONAIA

Galataki

Solygeia

Cleonae
(Kondostavlos)

Cleonae

Herakleion

Chiliomoudi

Athicia

Sophico

Nemea

Ag. Vassilios

Tenea

Klenia

Korphos

Venakia

Ag. Ioannis

Tretos Mt.

Stephani

Aghionori

Agelocastro

Mycenae

Limnes

Arachnaion Mt.

Part of the agora of Ancient Corinth, with the archaic temple on the levelled area of high ground.

TOPOGRAPHIC DESCRIPTION OF ANCIENT CORINTHIA

In ancient times, the heights of Geraneia marked the border separating Corinthia from the Megarid. A mountainous road led through the modern resort of Loutraki to Megara via the Megarian township of Tripodiskoi (now Megalo Derveni). But even in those times the main road to Megara was the coastal road that crossed the Scironian rocks, the modern equivalent of which is the road connecting Aghioi Theodoroi-Kinetta-Kaki Skala.

The first Corinthian town encountered by a visitor from Megara was Krommyon, at Aghioi Theodoroi. According to mythology, the inland area of Krommyon was the hunting-ground of the wild boar that Theseus killed on his journey from the Isthmus to Athens.

The next noteworthy settlement was Schoinous (near modern Kalamaki), and between the two there was a spot called Sidous which is mentioned, together with Krommyon, in the history of the Peloponnesian War. Schoinous was the starting-point of a paved-road (the *diolkos*) which the Corinthians had built for the purpose of drawing ships across (the verb *dielko* meaning to draw across) from the Corinthian to the Saronic gulf, and vice-versa. Sections of this road, still bearing visible marks of the wheeled vehicle that conveyed the ships across the Isthmus, were excavated on either side of the canal especially at its west end. The road did not follow a straight line, which explains why its length exceeded the width of the Isthmus (6 km.).

Near the hot springs of the modern spa of Loutraki, there existed a small settlement named *Therma*. There was another more important settlement within the area of the Heraion of Perachora, similarly named *Heraion*, and further north (in the direction of village Asprocambos), probably, there was yet another, known as *Peiraion*; all three of these — Therma, Heraion and Peiraion — were mentioned by Xenophon in his description of Agesilaus' military operations during 390 B.C. Following the excavations at Perachora, it has often been put forward that the name Peiraion, meaning the settlement "on the other side" or "across the way", had been given to the settlement by the Megarians, who were masters of the area before the rise of Corinth. The Megarians, of course, could only describe as being "on the other side" or "across the way" a position or settlement that was situated south of the Isthmus, probably in the area of Poseidon's sanctuary at Isthmia. This obviously conflicts with the toponyms in use at the time of the Corinthian war, as they have become known to us through Xenophon, for whom Peiraion was the settlement opposite Corinth, corresponding to the modern village of Perachora.

From Schoinous, the ancient road led to Cenchreae, the eastern port of Corinth, passing through the *sanctuary of Poseidon at Isthmia*, the place where the Isthmian Games (one of the four Panhellenic Festivals) were celebrated every two years. The sanctuary has been excavated on the site now occupied by the village of Kyravryssi. In the port of Cenchreae there have also been recent excavations of the remains of late Roman and early Christian buildings, which archaeologists have long known to be lying there. At the southern extremity of the bay of Cenchreae, there still exists an ancient salt water spring, known in ancient times as the *Baths of Helen*. This name has been given to the small village now occupying the site. Further south, on the eminence occupied by the village of Galataki, a sanctuary was discovered which is believed to have belonged to the township of *Solygeia,* mentioned by Thucydides at the time of the Peloponnesian war (during which period it had apparently already fallen into decline).

From Cenchreae, the road climbed uphill to *Corinth,* situated on the spot now occupied by the modern village of Palia Corinthos, on the northern slopes of Acrocorinth. There was also a small settlement on the spot now occupied by Nea Corinthos; however, between Nea and Palia Corinthos (New and Old Corinth), at a place on the coast known as *Korakou,* excavations have brought to light the most important Mycenaean settlement of the entire area. In Lechaion, the northern port of Corinth, only a few pre-Christian remains were found, but excavations have revealed a large early Christian basilica.

The road running almost parallel to the coast west of ancient Corinth and Lechaion eventually led to *Sicyon.* Before the Hellenistic period, Sicyon was situated in the fertile, flat area between the villages of Kiato and Vassiliko; Vassiliko has now taken the name of Sicyon. During and after Hellenistic times, Sicyon was situated on the plateau of Vassiliko, which was formerly occupied by the acropolis. The port of Sicyon was always situated on the coast of Kiato. The coastal stretch west of Kiato, extending to the mouth of the river Sythas, near Xylocastro, also belonged to Sicyonia.

From Sicyon there was a mountainous road leading south; running along the

Long walls connected the city wall of Corinth with its northern harbour, Lechaion. Lechaion was largerly an artificial harbour deepened by excavation. The drawing shows the long walls, the site of the agora of Corinth, the Asklepieion, and also the walls of Acrocorinth and the sanctuary of Demeter and Kore.

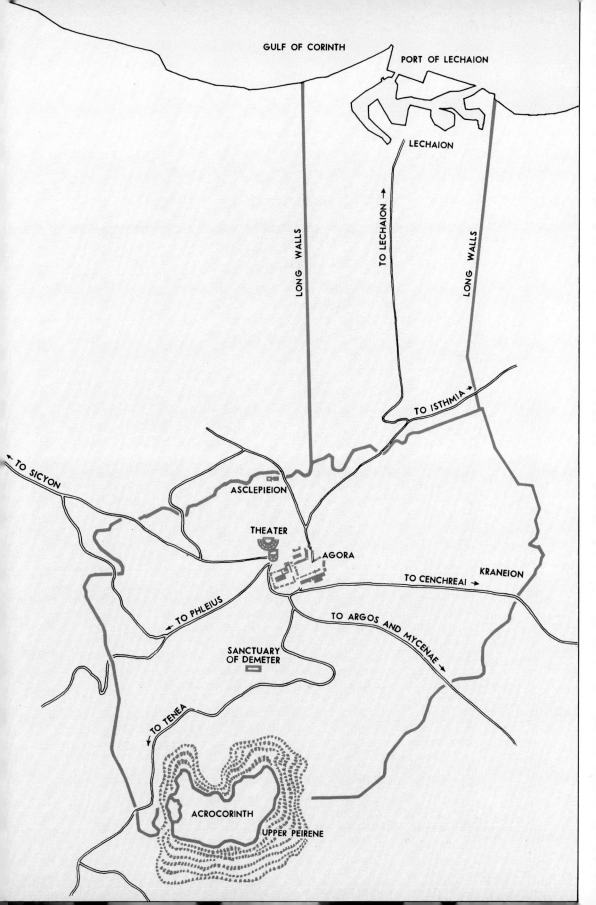

Painted clay metopes of the early archaic temple at Thermon in Aetolia are the earliest examples of Corinthian painting. The piece illustrated depicts the tragic heroine Chelidon (Athens, National Archaeological Museum).

western bank of the river Asopos, it ended up at *Phlius,* via *Titane.* The fortified acropolis of Titane still survives on a hill topped by an old chapel and the cemetery of the village Voivoda, now renamed Titane.

Going down into the plain of Nemea, the ancient road first went through *Phlius* — where meagre remains of the ancient theatre and a few public buildings belonging to the agora are now being excavated — and then led to the east of the village Koutsi, very near the modern highway connecting Sicyon and Nemea. The present village of Nemea (formerly Aghios Georghios) is situated in the ancient plain of Phlius, which was celebrated for its fine wines. It would have been more accurate to name it Phlius rather than Nemea.

Ancient *Nemea* lies about five kilometers south-east of modern Nemea, on the site now occupied by the village officially bearing the name of Ancient Nemea. In antiquity, Nemea was a small settlement belonging to Cleonae (and later to Argos).

Cleonae was situated in the plain between the villages of Kontostavlos and Aghios Vassilios; all that has survived of it is some meagre remains of the walls and, in a better condition, the foundations of Herakles' sanctuary outside the walls, on the western side of the city, now at a short distance left of the public highway connecting Kontostavlos to Aghios Vassilios. The village of Kontostavlos has been renamed Cleonae, although it lies at some distance north-west of

Wooden votive tablet found, together with other similar ones, in the cave of Pitsa, near Corinth. A rare specimen of Greek painting in the Archaic period (540 B.C.), it represents a sacrificial scene. To the right is the altar which the worshippers approach with their offerings. A small boy leads the sacrificial animal (a lamb). All the participants are crowned with garlands in accordance with ritual ceremony.

the ancient city. Not so far from Cleonae, at a place known as *Zygouries,* a prehistoric settlement has been excavated. The ancient road from Cleonae led towards Mycenae and Argos, passing through the Dervenakia pass. Another road led from Nemea to Mycenae and Argos, bypassing Dervenakia. The Argives had built a fortified watch-tower as a check-point (which has survived in good condition) just before the road joins up with the main road after the Dervenakia pass (to the right of the main road and near Mycenae).

There are very few visible vestiges of *Tenea* in the flat and fertile area between the villages of Chiliomodi and Klenia, now crossed by the modern highway which leads up from Chiliomodi to *Klenia,* and thence to Aghionori, where one can see a well-preserved medieval fortress. From Aghionori, the road descends to Argos via the villages of Limnes, Prosymna and Chonikas. The same course was followed in antiquity by a rough mountainous road (''kontoporeia'', meaning ''short cut''), which was taken in preference to the other road by travellers wishing to go from Argos to Corinth without crossing the Dervenakia pass.

The border between Corinthia and Achaia was the river *Sythas,* now known as the Trikalian river (or the river of Xylocastro, because its mouth is near that village). To the south, Corinthia extended to the northern slopes of Mounts Tretos and Arachnaion.

The Isthmus, the sole bridge connecting mainland Greece with the Peloponnese. The plan to cut a canal through it was conceived as early as the Archaic period, but was only implemented in modern times (1881-1893).

CORINTH AND CORINTHIA

The Isthmus has always been the only bridge connecting mainland Greece to the Peloponnesus, a peninsula larger than the whole of central Greece as far up north as Thessaly.

There were two considerable advantages to be gained by settling near this natural bridge; but these could easily turn to disadvantages, which is what happened in the case of Corinth on various occasions. The two advantages were the following: a settlement placed in such a position could draw important benefits from controlling the passage across the Isthmus; at the same time, such a settlement could found its economy on the exploitation of the two seas on either side of the Isthmus and on active relations with trade centres east and west. The first advantage rapidly turned into a disadvantage, owing to the multitude of peoples who moved south, since mythical times, in search of a permanent abode in the Peloponnesus. Groups of invaders in varying numbers went through Corinth and kept the entire area in a constant state of turmoil, hindering its political and economical development. This is the reason why Homer refers to Corinth as a minor provincial centre, politically dependant on the kingdom of Agamemnon. The second advantage proved more profitable, but only for a brief period in the long history of Corinth: the period that was to become known as the golden age

Kenchreai. Remains of buildings and fortifications, dating from the end of the ancient world. The north mole at the entrance of the harbour.

of Corinth, beginning about two centuries after the assimilation of the Dorians and ending with the Persian wars. Corinth's conflict with naval powers sharing the same interests marked the end of her ascendancy.

Pre-Dorian Corinth

It has been established that during the 4th millennium there existed a small Neolithic settlement on the exact site which Corinth occupied during the historical era. The water of the Peirene spring and the natural fortification provided by the neighbouring hill of Acrocorinth probably led that rural population to settle on that site. They must have been several small settlements scattered throughout the area, just as they are known to have existed in the following period — the Bronze Age. There are at least eight Bronze Age settlements known to us, extending from Isthmia and Cenchreae to Corinth. Some of these have been excavated, like the settlement of Korakou (on the coastal stretch between Nea Corinthos and Lechaion), which was more important than Corinth in Mycenaean times. Before 1800 B.C., many peoples from the East settled in the area, especially Phoenicians, as indicated by the fact that the most representative deity of Corinth in historical times was the Phoenician Aphrodite. Aeolian tribes from Thessaly also descended occasionally upon the Peloponnesus to settle permanently. (There is a myth according to which Endymion reached Corinthia at the head of an Aeolian group, but found there was no room left for them, and so was forced to proceed to Elis.) The Dorians who had settled in Doris were not able or willing to invade Attica in order to reach the Isthmus through the Megarid, which was a province of Attica at that time. They preferred to cross over to the Peloponnesus by Rhion-Antirrhion and invade first Arcadia and subsequently settle in the Argolid. From the Argolid, as explicitly mentioned by Thucydides (4,42), they entered Corinthia, the "dorization" of which is supposed to have begun in 900 B.C. It is believed nowadays that prior to conquering Corinthia, the Dorians invaded the Megarid via the Isthmus (which marked the beginning of the Megarid) and took it away from the Athenians. After they had also conquered Corinthia, two new Dorian states came into being (Megara and Corinth) which differed in many aspects from the metropolitan Dorian state of Argos; one of these differences was ethnological, since the former population of both settlements was not the same as in Argos. The cult of the Argive Hera was transferred at an early date to the Heraion of Perachora, which was to become one of the most venerable sanctuaries of the Corinthians in historical times.

The rise of Corinth

In the 8th century B.C., the Corinthians founded two important colonies in the West, Corcyra and Syracuse. (According to traditional sources, both these colonies already existed in 730 or 720 B.C.) The reason usually given for this expansion was the flourishing economic position of Corinth in the 8th century B.C. However, archaeologists and scholars have searched in vain among the results of excavations for indications of wealth or economic prosperity during the 8th century B.C. (for instance, opulent buildings or works of art). For this reason, Corinth's early colonization in the West might be ascribed more correctly to the unusual increase of population resulting from the Dorian settling in the preceding century. The foundation of the two colonies led to a rapid growth of the economy, thanks to a more active navigation and intensified exports of handicraft to the West. This also helped, at a very early date, to raise the artistic standard of Corinth, as we can see in the proto-Corinthian and Corinthian vases, the painted tablets of an archaic Corinthian sanctuary, the inscribed metopes of Thermos, the famous chest of Cypselus, and the early development of bronze-craft. These were the foundations on which the naval and economic power of Corinth was built and maintained until the Persian wars.

At the very beginning of historical times, under the rule of Pheidon or perhaps earlier still, the Dorians of Argos liked to boast about the glorious past of their country, appropriating all the myths and glory of Mycenae and Tiryns and honouring the local Achaean sovereigns as their own heroes. The aristocratic Dorian families of Corinth attempted to do the same; but in Mycenaean times, Corinth was simply a province of Agamemnon's kingdom, like Sicyon, Cleonae and other Corinthian towns (Iliad, B 570-576), in spite of the fact that it was much wealthier than Mycenae and could trace its beginnings far back into the past, as indicated by the pre-Hellenic form of the toponym Corinth. It is for this reason that as early perhaps as the 8th century B.C. the Dorians of Corinth appropriated the myths of Ephyra, which Homer refers to as lying in the "deepest recess of horse-grazing Argos", meaning the inland area of the Argive plain, where prehistoric remains were excavated (in the Nemea and Cleonae area, which had once formed part of Corinthian territory). The sovereigns Homer mentions in Ephyra are Sisyphus, his son Glaucus and Glaucus' son

Coin of Sicyon depicting a chimaera. Inscription: SE (KYON). Corinthian coins. The one (on the left) has a representation of Pegasos, and that (on the right) portrays Athena.

Bellerophon, who had a close relationship with Proitos, king of Tyrins, and was sent by him to Lycia (Iliad, Z 152-170). Sisyphus and Bellerophon were considered local heroes in Corinth, and Pegasus, the winged horse tamed by Bellerophon (for which exploit he became famous in Asia Minor), came to be accepted as a Corinthian emblem, and remained so until the end of antiquity. Eumelos, a Corinthian poet only slightly posterior to Homer, a member of the aristocratic Dorian family of the Bacchiads, had an active hand in reshaping these ancient myths and linking them up with the Thessalian myths centering around Jason and Medea. None of Eumelos' works had survived in advanced historical times; but he had a decisive influence on the living oral tradition of the Corinthians.

Corinth in Classical and Hellenistic times

In the 5th century B.C., Corinth was one of the three major powers in Greece, and took part in all the battles against the Persians both on land and at sea. After the Persians ceased to be a danger to Greece, it was inevitable that Corinth should come into conflict with the relatively more recent and powerful naval force that was Athens. Corinth was the main instigator of the Peloponnesian war. However, in spite of its favourable outcome, as far as the alliance was concerned, this war did not ensure naval supremacy for Corinth. On the contrary, it raised Sparta to the rank of the first power in Greece. This led the frustrated Corinth to give up once and for all her dreams of naval supremacy, to start an alliance with Athens and other discontented cities, and to launch the Corinthian war, proclaiming that her purpose was to free the Greek cities from

Spartan hegemony. But soon after this, the new power from the North and the secret intentions of king Philip II to control the political life of the entire country led the principal cities of Greece to unite in their opposition to him. After Philip's victory in 338 and the general recognition of his leadership in the offensive against the Persians, he was the first among the Macedonian sovereigns to set up a garrison in Acrocorinth. His example was followed by the Antigonids on several occasions until 243 B.C., when Aratos, as general of the Achaean League, seized the fortress and handed it over to the Corinthians, who then joined the League. About a century later, at a time when the Romans had begun to take an interest in Greek politics, Corinth had become the capital city of the League, and as such the Romans took their revenge upon it by destroying it completely (146 B.C.).

The Roman period and the years that followed it

A hundred years later, Julius Caesar introduced a project for the reconstruction of destroyed cities, which he intended colonizing with veteran soldiers and landless subjects from the great Roman cities. Corinth was among the cities due for reconstruction; colonization began in 44 B.C. During that year, Caesar was assassinated and reconstruction was continued and completed under the Emperor Augustus. The first public buildings were erected by the state. For centuries later, Corinth was designated on coins as *Colonia Laus Julia Corinthus* (Julia because it was founded by the patrician family of the Julii, of which both Caesar and Augustus were members). In addition to the Roman settlers, a number of emancipated Greeks from Rome were given land in Corinth or encouraged to settle there. Several tradesmen, seamen and businessmen from the East — especially from Egypt — also came to settle in Corinth. Latin was the official language, but only for a relatively brief period (most Latin inscriptions discovered in Corinth belong to the first century of the Christian era). The continuous increase of the Greek element in the population brought about a simultaneous use of the Greek language and eventually the abandonment of Latin. The cosmopolitan character of Corinth also affected its religious life. Cults of all kinds were practised in perfect freedom, and diverse rites mingled and co-existed, inevitably infuencing each other. The situation was the same in the ports of Cenchreae and Lechaion, which had become the permanent abode of many foreign merchants. In A.D. 52, the Apostle Paul found the ground propitious for his preaching; during that year he was able to establish an important Christian church in Cenchreae. During the 2nd and 3rd centuries A.D., several emperors and wealthy individuals took an interest in the improvement of the city, its suburbs and ports. Among the oldest benefactors of Corinth were Eurycles, who built some fine baths, and Babbius Philinus who embellished the agora with the well-known round, monopteral (with a single row of columns) structure. During the 1st century A.D., the Emperor Nero began to carry out his plans for opening up the Isthmus. In the 2nd century the Emperor Hadrian showed his interest in Corinth by building an aqueduct, while Herod Atticus embellished the Corinthian agora and the sanctuary of Isthmian Poseidon. The early Christian community of Corinth and the neighbouring ports built a number of monumental structures. Best known are the large basilicas of Lechaion, Cenchreae and Craneion. Towards the middle of the 3rd century A.D., when hordes of bar-

Bronze mirrors. The discs are supported by korai. From Corinthian workshops (Athens, National Archaeological Museum).

barians began to invade the Roman provinces, the wealth of Corinth inevitably attracted the majority of the invaders. In the 6th century A.D. the Emperor Justinian displayed considerable concern for the safety of Corinth, building the trans-Isthmian wall, several sections of which have survived to this day with a good deal of later restoration work. The construction of this wall entailed pulling down many pre-Christian structures (already in ruins at the time), particularly the sanctuary of Isthmian Poseidon, which was the point where the wall began, ending up on the coast of the Corinthian gulf, on the east outskirts of Nea Corinthos. However, the practical use of this wall (which became known as the six-mile wall, as it was 7.3 kilometers long, i.e. just under six Roman miles) was very limited.

The vicissitudes of Corinth during the middle ages and four centuries of Turkish rule were the natural consequences of the strategic importance of Acrocorinth, which repeatedly changed hands during this long period. Its successive rulers occasionally repaired and renovated the fortifications. Shortly before the Franks occupied Greece, Leo Sgouros, sovereign of Nauplia, and his garrison were able to delay the surrender of the fortress by putting up a stout resistance. Acrocorinth remained in the hands of both Frankish and Greek sovereigns until 1458, when it was finally occupied by the Turks. However, Turkish rule was interrupted, when the Knights of Malta (1612) and the Venetians (1687) laid claim to the fortress and held it for a time. The Turkish forces that occupied it during the Greek War of Independence were forced by the Greeks' military success to evacuate it as early as 1822, resuming only a temporary hold on it in the immediately following years. During the War of Independance, and for some time after it, there had been some thoughts of making Corinth the capital of Greece, because of its exceptional position at the very heart of the revolutionary turmoil. However, Athens was inevitably believed to have closer and more obvious links with the glories of the past and was therefore chosen as the capital in 1834. A preference for Corinth was excluded once and for all after the great earthquake of 1858, which completely destroyed the small town that had survived centuries of Turkish occupation and had started to be restored since 1829 on the site of the ancient city. After the earthquake, it was decided to build the new town nearer to the Isthmus, but it was destroyed once again by the earthquakes of 1928. Reconstruction started at once and progressed rapidly until one of the Greece's most attractive towns — Corinth as we now know it — came into being. The small village occupying the site of ancient Corinth has similarly been reconstructed and improved.

SICYON, CLEONAE AND NEMEA

Sicyon is undoubtedly the most important among the other cities of ancient Corinthia. Sicyon retained clearer signs than Corinth of its former dependance on Agamemnon's kingdom or the pre-Dorian Argolid: king Adrastos, compelled to abandon Argos, took refuge in Sicyon and became its ruler (Iliad B 572). He was later honoured in Sicyon as a hero, until the local ruler Cleisthenes, moved by hostility towards the Argives, put an end to the honours rendered to the Argive hero (Herodotus, 5, 67).

Sicyon was built in a fertile plain and reached the peak of its prosperity about the same time as Corinth — the 7th and 6th centuries B.C. — when political power was yielded by the aristocratic family of the Orthagorids. The most famous member of this family was Cleisthenes (circa 580 B.C.), whose daughter

View of the agora from the acropolis of Hellenistic Sicyon. The orchestra of the theatre can be seen, as well as the lower rows of seats and the foundations of the skene. Beyond it is the Roman bath, nowadays used as a museum.

Agariste married the Alcmeonid Megacles in Athens; her son, also named Cleisthenes, was the reformer of Athenian government. (Pericles belonged to the same family.) The golden age of Sicyon lasted until the early 5th century B.C. In the Peloponnesian and Corinthian wars, Sicyon fought on the side of Sparta. Some efforts were made to establish democracy in Sicyon, but the results were not encouraging and only lasted for a limited time.

In the 4th and 3rd centuries B.C., Sicyon was ruled by oligarchs or tyrants. In 303 B.C. it fell into the hands of Demetrius Poliorcetes; with the assent of the inhabitans he built the new city on the tableland where the village of Vassiliko is now situated. When the new city was finished, most of the Sicyonians abandoned the plain lying between Vassiliko and Kiato, which was the site of the archaic and classical city. However, the harbour, which used to be where Kiato now stands, continued to operate as a fairly important neighbourhood. The new city continued to be ruled by tyrants, each of whom succesively exterminated his opponent or rival to seize power, until 251 B.C., when Aratos of Sicyon, who later distinguished himself as a general of the Achaean League, freed the city and made it a member of the alliance.

Nemea and Cleonae were nearer to Argos and were therefore compelled to throw in their fortunes with those of the Argives. The area occupied by the sanctuary of Nemea belonged to Cleonae, and that was where the Cleoneans held the Panhellenic Nemean games. In later times, the organization of these games was taken over by the Argives.

In contrast, Phlius remained a staunch ally of Sparta and an enemy to the neighbouring Argives, who missed no opportunity of taking their revenge on the inhabitants by repeatedly plandering the city and the surrounding land.

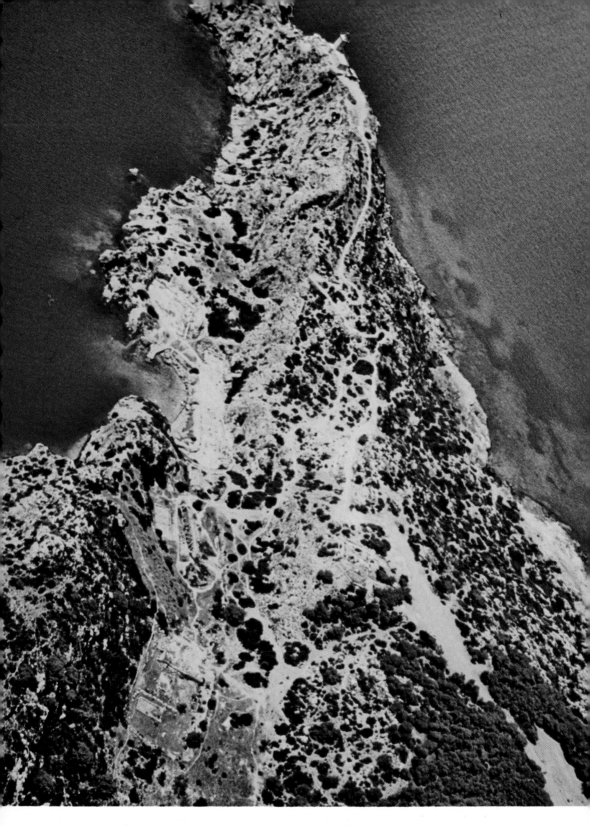

Aerial view of the Heraion at Perachora.

EXCAVATIONS

THE HERAION OF PERACHORA

The sanctuary of Hera and the area immediately surrounding it were excavated and studied by the British School of Archaeology from 1930 to 1933. Research on a smaller scale was carried out in the following years up to this day. The Heraion occupied the western point of the Perachora peninsula lying opposite Corinth and Kiato; it can be reached by land from Loutraki, which is about 10 kilometers from Perachora. The distance from Perachora to the Heraion is slightly longer. The sanctuary was built in the hollow of a small port south-east of the rocks upon which now stands the lighthouse. On the lighthouse promontory one can still see some vestiges of the fortifications surrounding the ancient settlement, which spread around the sanctuary and further inland, in the direction of the lake Vouliagmeni.

It is believed that the sanctuary was founded in the early 8th century B.C. by Dorian Argives who had enlarged their sovereignty during the preceding century to include Corinthia and the Megarid. Some scholars believe that it was founded by the Argives of Megara and initially belonged to them rather than to Corinth. However the case may be, it is certain that the sanctuary came under Corinthian rule within the 8th century B.C. Votive inscriptions tell us that the temple, which stood very near the port, was dedicated to Hera Akraia (*akron* is the extremity of

The Heraion at Perachora. The foundations of the temple, dedicated to Hera Akraia, can be seen, as well as the altar and a stoa near the harbour.

the peninsula); there was also an apsidal temple belonging to the Geometric period. Another temple was built on the same spot in the Archaic period, seven meters west of the geometric temple. Further inland, about 200 meters east-wards, a second sanctuary was excavated; from an inscribed 6th century jar it became known that it belonged to Hera Limenia (of the port). There were doubts as to whether this second sanctuary included a temple. The edifice that was discovered (only the foundations have survived) was supposed to have served as a place for performing religious rites and sheltering votive offerings, of which a large number were brought to light during the excavations. Between the two sanctuaries, the excavators discovered a stoa (arcade) in the shape of the letter gamma (Γ). To the east, over a large expanse of land, one can see vestiges of water-cisterns hewn into the rock, foundations of houses and walls, and buttres-ses. They all belonged to the settlement that had developed around the sanctuary and that also went by the name of Heraion.

Plan of the Heraion at Perachora and surrounding area.

Reconstruction of the stoa at the Heraion of Perachora. The stoa was excavated near the harbour and belongs to the two shrines of Hera (Akraia and Limenia). It is L-shaped and dates from the end of the 5th or beginning of the 4th century B.C.

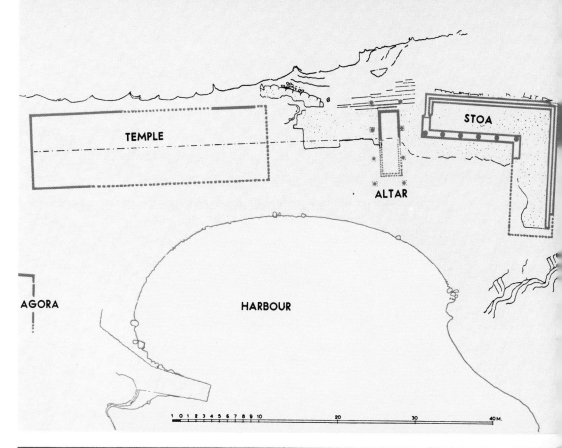

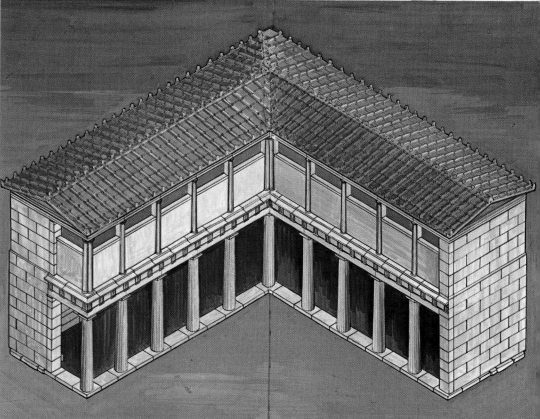

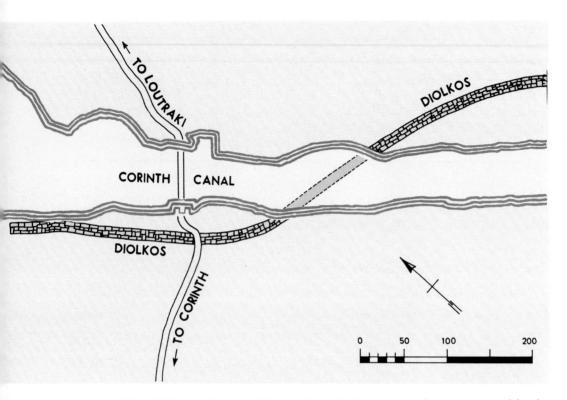

The 1956 excavation revealed part of the diolkos, the paved way constructed by the Corinthians so that boats could be hauled across ("dielkein") from the Corinthian Gulf to the Saronic and vice versa.

THE DIOLKOS

In 1956 and later, the Ephor N. Verdelis excavated a section of the paved road built by the tyrants of Corinth to connect the Saronic coast to the Corinthian in order to haul ships over from the one sea to the other. The excavation of this section (near the west end of the modern canal) revealed that the paved road was used as a passage for a wheeled vehicle upon which the ship was strapped after having been relieved of its cargo. The road was known by the technical term *diolkos*, from the verb *dielko* meaning "to haul across". The wheeled vehicle used for hauling was known as ὁλκὸς νεῶν, meaning "hauler of ships". The width of the diolkos varied between 3 to 5.5 meters.

The Corinthians planned to cut a canal through the Isthmus from the period of the tyrants, but this ambitious project was continually deferred on account of the technical difficulties and great expense involved. A temporary solution was sought in the construction of a paved way, which gave some assistance to shipping, though only on a limited scale. It was particularly useful for transporting war-ships, which did not have a cargo. Merchant ships had to dock at Kenchreai and unload their cargo before being transported over the diolkos to the Corinthian gulf. The cargo was carried overland to Lechaion, where the boat put in for reloading. Clearly the loading and unloading were expensive.

Remains of the diolkos at the Corinthian Isthmus. The deep parallel grooves, 1.5 m. apart, were for the wheels of the device for transporting the ships. By this paved road ships were dragged from the Saronic to Corinthian Gulf.

THE CANAL

The cutting of a canal through the Isthmus had been planned as early as the time of Periander, but no attempt was made to implement the scheme. The canal was later planned by Demetrios Poliorketes, though again it was not put into practice. Studies of it were undertaken by Julius Caesar, and the Emperors Gaius (Caligula) and Hadrian. Gaius sent men to the Isthmus in about A.D. 40 to study the scheme on the spot. An opinion delivered by Egyptians had a restraining effect; they discovered that the level of the Corinthian gulf was higher than that of the Saronic, and declared that the cutting of the canal would result in the inundation of Aigina.

The most important attempt to pierce the Isthmus in ancient times was made by the Emperor Nero in A.D. 67. During that year, several thousands of workmen dug away at the Isthmus for more than three months. The vestiges of the work carried out at that time indicate that the designers of the project had chosen the narrowest point of the Isthmus for the purpose, following the same line as the modern canal. The digging began on either side of the Isthmus, and the workmen were supposed to meet eventually in the middle. Nero's death put an end to the project. Work was only resumed again in 1881 and completed in 1893. The canal is about 6 kilometers long, its width upon completion (when first came to use) was about 25 meters (21 at the bottom), and the water 8 meters deep.

THE SANCTUARY OF ISTHMIA

The sanctuary of Isthmian Poseidon, where the Panhellenic Isthmian games were held every two years, was excavated between 1952 and 1960 at the village of Kyravryssi, south of the modern bridge of the canal and near the southern end of it, at Isthmia. The remains of the first temple of Poseidon (the groundwork was 40×14 meters, and there was a peristyle of wooden columns) has been dated as belonging to the 7th century B.C. The foundations of an elongated altar (considerably larger than the width of the east side of the temple's platform) were discovered east of the temple. Other discoveries included votive offerings of the Archaic period (clay and bronze statuettes, fragments of marble sculptures from the time of Cypselus and Periandros).

Not long before the mid-5th century B.C., this temple had already been replaced by another temple, also peripteral, but made of stone, with columns 6×13 (stylobate 54×23 meters). This second temple was burnt during the Corinthian war (390 B.C.), when Agesilaus fought in the area against the Corinthians and their Argive allies, and also against the Athenians under Iphicrates (Xen. Hell. 4, 5, 4). The temple was restored on the same architectural plan, and survived till the final destruction of Corinth in 146 B.C.

When the reconstruction of Corinth began in 44 B.C., the various structures of the sanctuary at Isthmia were also renovated. The temple was rebuilt with the

Aerial view of the sanctuary at Isthmia. The canal and the Saronic Gulf can be seen in the background.

same dimensions of the cella, but probably (in this or in a later restoration) it became amphiprostyle temple, without outer rows of columns. This explains why Pausanias in the second century A.D. described it as a not very large temple (ναὸς μέγεθος οὐ μείζων).

A marble perirrhanterion of the seventh century B.C. belongs to the ancient temple of Poseidon; it was now on exhibition in the archaeological collection housed in the area of Isthmia.

The sanctuary of Poseidon had a perimeter wall with an entrance both on the side facing Krommyon and on that towards Corinth. During the second century B.C. the sanctuary was extended, and stoas were constructed on all sides, facing towards the temple. There was a propylon in the south-east corner of the sanctuary during the final phase, which may have served as the main entrance to the shrine, used by those arriving overland from Attica.

To the east of the temple there are fragments of a long narrow altar near which animal bones were found amongst ash, fragments of archaic pottery, and iron and bronze objects. This was probably therefore the site of the Archaic period altar.

The foundations have been preserved of the altar of the Classical period, which was also to the east of the building. The altar was destroyed and abandoned during the early Roman period, as can be deduced from traces of wheels on the roads for carriages that passed above it. It was later rebuilt 19 m. to the east, only to be destroyed again before the end of the Roman period.

The sanctuary at Isthmia. The wall across the Isthmus is marked, as is the earlier Cyclopean wall and the main buildings of the sanctuary.

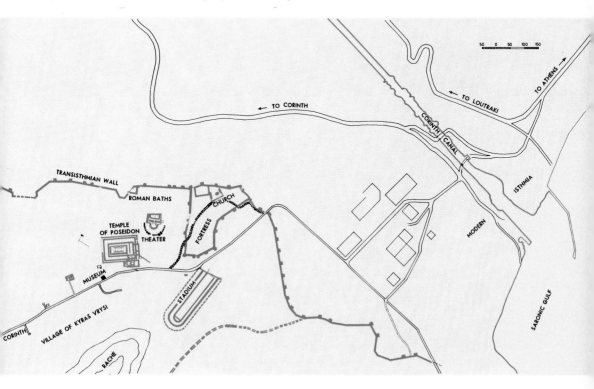

The temple and sanctuary of Poseidon at Isthmia. The Palaimonion can be seen in the upper left corner, behind the stoa.

Reconstruction of the Palaimonion, based on Corinthian coins.

Palaimonion

In Roman times, the old stadium situated beyond the south-east corner of Poseidon's sanctuary fell into disuse; this made room for the foundation of a temple and enclosure dedicated to Palaimon. According to tradition, the Isthmian games were celebrated in honour of the boy Palaimon, son of king Athamas and Ino; his corpse was washed ashore near Isthmia on a dolphin's back. A round structure encircled with columns, often represented on Corinthian coins during the Imperial era, had been described long ago as the "temple of Palaimon". Inside this structure there is a dolphin carrying the body of the dead Palaimon. It is believed that the building stood upon a heavy platform (8.3 × 7.7 meters) unearthed at the southern end of the old stadium which was the starting-point for the races. There was an *adyton* possibly used only for secret rites, under the platform of the temple, to which one had access through an entrance on the east side of the temple.

Plutarch gives a hint about the mystic rites, which are supplemented by large numbers of peculiar lamps, larger than usual in size, which have been unearthed during the latest excavations. A good number of them are on exhibition in the Museum at Isthmia. These lamps were used to illuminate the *adyton* or innermost sanctuary, and the secret corridor that led down to it, which was in darkness. Palaimon was also associated with the sacred pine tree which grew near to his altar.

Reconstruction of the shrine of Palaimon, and the gate that connected it with the sanctuary of Poseidon.

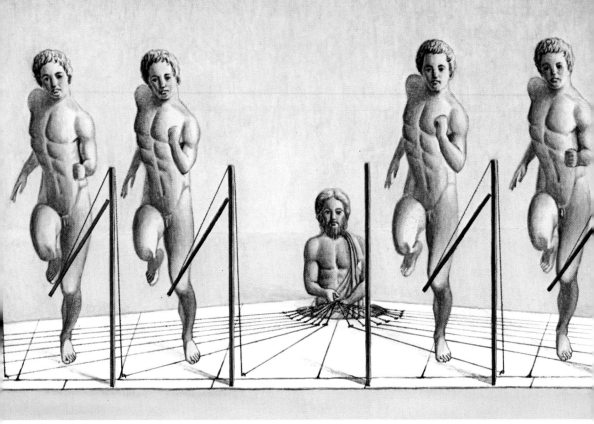

Reconstruction of the starting gate at the Isthmia. It is shaped like an isosceles triangle, with a circular pit at the apex in which the starter stood. When he released the ropes, the horizontal bars all fell simultaneously.

The stadium

All that has survived of the classical stadium is a section of the triangular starting-point of the race-track, paved with poros stone slabs. This discovery has enabled scholars to study the special system in force at Isthmia for starting off the runners.

The later stadium (used during the Hellenistic and Roman periods) was situated at a small distance south of the sanctuary, at the foot of a hillock named Rachi; a natural hollow made this spot eminently suitable for a stadium. A little digging soon revealed the starting-point and finishing-point of the race-track, which made it possible to determine the length of the one-stadium race at Isthmia (181.15 meters, whereas at Olympia it was 192.27 m., at Delphi approximately 178 m. and at the Panathenian stadium 184.96 m.).

The games held at Isthmia (the Isthmian Games) were originally of a local character. They were later reorganised by the tyrants, however, and assumed a panhellenic nature. The Corinthians were responsible for the organisation of them, just as the Eleans organised the Olympic games. They were suspended after the destruction of Corinth in 146 B.C., but the responsibility for organising them was quickly assumed by Sicyon. With the rebuilding of Corinth in 44 B.C., the games were reorganised, and the sanctuary at Isthmia was reconstructed and

Partial view of the foundations of the various buildings of the sanctuary at Isthmia. The old stadium start, can be seen, as well as the propylon and the Saronic Gulf in the background.

enriched with new buildings. The games were held every two years and were of great importance. While they were taking place, the "Isthmian Truce" was observed between the Corinthians and the other Greek states.

The theatre

The cavea of the theatre, the supporting walls of the side-entrances and the scene building were pulled apart in the early Christian period to give stones for the trans-Isthmian wall. Only a few vestiges have remained of the Roman stage structure, the side-entrances, which were apparently roofed with barrel vaults and the front seats in the cavea. It is believed that efforts were made to enlarge the cavea during Nero's visit in A.D. 67 by building piers as supports under the rows of seats, as was the custom in Roman times. Behind the stage there was an enclosed space, which according to some scholars included an inner peristyle and a colonnade that could be used as guest-rooms during the games.

Before the Roman period, at one stage of the Hellenistic history of the theatre, there is reason to believe that the seats were divided into four central sections, made up of curved, tiered rows, and two sections at either end (one by each side-entrance) made up of straight rows of seats, vertical to the proscenium.

Mosaic floor, recently discovered in the Roman bath at the sanctuary at Isthmia by the American School of Classical Studies under professor P. Clement. The floor has decorative motifs framing the two central pictures. Tritons and Nereides in a sea scape.
(Right) Part of the floor with the two pictures. Detail of the central motif.
(Left) Detail of one of the two pictures from the mosaic floor.

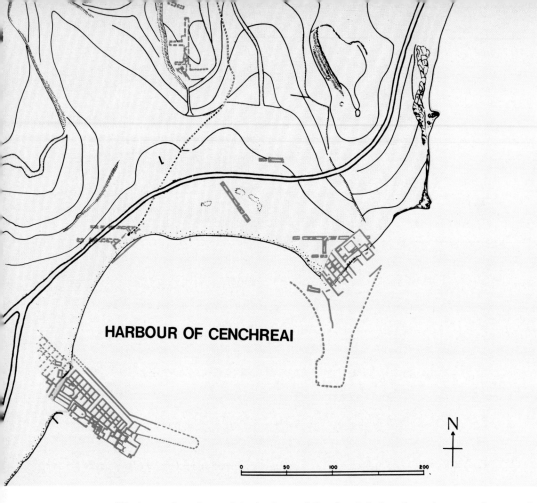

HARBOUR OF CENCHREAI

N

The horse-shoe shape of the harbour of Cenchreai derives from the two moles opposite each other. The south mole was the more important, and housed harbour instalations, the shrine of Isis, and later the Early Christian basilica that replaced it. The shrine of Aphrodite may have been on the north mole.

THE PORTS OF CORINTH

CENCHREAE

Corinth's east port was situated in the first inlet south of Isthmia, which is still known as the bay of Cenchreae, after a village by that name at a small distance from the coast. During the Roman imperial period, there was a series of porticoes standing along the half-moon recess of the bay, as indicated by representations of the port on old Corinthian coins. There were various structures on both the piers that extended into the sea at the north and south end of the port. The south pier was the widest. Excavations have brought to light the foundations of the structures on land, and there has been research on some of the structures that have sunk into the sea. Among these structures there was a temple of Isis and further out an early Christian basilica. At the inland extremity of the north pier there are the ruins of a tower and further the foundations of mudbrick structures of the late Roman and early Christian periods.

The harbour of Cenchreai is seldom referred to by ancient authors, despite

Aerial view of Cenchreai. The foundations of the south mole can be seen, submerged beneath the sea. As with the whole of the Peloponnesian coastline, the sea is higher than in antiquity, and many coastal buildings of ancient times are therefore now below sea-level.

the fact that it was of some importance for Corinthian communications with the East and the Greek islands.

The Apostle Paul makes mention of a very early Christian community at Cenchreai in his epistle to the Romans. In this same epistle he introduces a deaconess to the Christians in Rome. This deaconess, whose name was Phoebe, received the letter from Paul himself at Corinth or at Cenchreai in the winter of A.D. 52-53, and took it with her to Rome. In the spring of this year (53) Paul took ship in the harbour of Cenchreai with his companions and left for Ephesos.

Merchandise from the entire eastern basin of the Mediterranean came to Cenchreai during the Roman period. The natural anchorage had been converted into an exceptionally fine harbour by the construction of moles, as early as the Hellenistic period. Most of the harbour buildings belong to the Roman period. At some points the foundations of them are visible, though most of them are now submerged under the sea. The south mole had a variety of installations, and a group of warehouses at the service of commerce.

Excavation began in 1963, funded by the American School and the Universities of Chicago and Indiana, and under the supervision of Professors Scranton

Reconstruction of the ware-houses. This complex of rooms of the south pier was obviously used for the varied merchandise brought to Cenchreai.

Part of the ancient foundations of the south mole at Cenchreai. On the right of the picture are the foundations of the Early Christian basilica. A small part only of the east side of the basilica is submerged beneath the sea.

and Ramage. Sub-aqua techniques were used for part of the exploration, and a variety of discoveries came to light, which are now housed in the archaeological collection at Isthmia.

Cenchreai appears to have suffered particularly badly from earthquakes, especially those of A.D. 365 and 375, when the greatest destruction occurred.

HELEN'S BATH

On the south fringe of the bay of Cenchreae, there is a small cluster of houses that has been given the name of Helen's bath. On the sea-shore nearby there is a salt-water spring that also existed in antiquity and was known in Roman times as Helen's bath. In ancient times the springwater formed a small stream, but nowadays it pours directly into the sea.

The spring is thought to have healing properties, because the temperature of the water used to be higher than average, and it is still slightly tepid today. In antiquity, the spring was one of the sights of Cenchreai. Thucydides uses the term "Reitoi" to describe the large number of mouths. In the Roman period the water appears to have been collected in a reservoir.

Lechaion, the northern harbour of Corinth, flourished in the late Roman and early christian period. Among the most important remains of the christian era are the foundations of an elongated Basilica, recently excavated. (Aerial view)

LECHAION

Lechaion, Corinth's northern port, was most important to the city in pre-Classical times. Even in later times, the Corinthians showed considerable interest in Lechaion, as it was the port nearest to their city. Most of the port was an artificial construction, the result of excavation and dredging. In the 5th century B.C., the Corinthians connected Corinth and Lechaion with long walls. There has been no systematic excavation or research of the port yet. Among other vestiges of late antiquity, the foundations of a large early Christian basilica (179 meters long) have been unearthed along the sea-front.

Foundations of the long walls have been discovered between Corinth and Lechaion. The sections that have been preserved seem to indicate that the lower courses of the walls were of limestone and the upper courses of brick. Lechaion was a spacious, secure harbour, thanks to the large-scale constructions that secured calm waters within it. According to Pausanias, there was a temple of Poseidon, and a bronze statue of the god, at Lechaion. Plutarch states that there was a sanctuary of Aphrodite there, in which sacrifices were made to the goddess.

Corinth

Part of the agora of Ancient Corinth, with the Northwest shops and the archaic temple in the background.
Ancient Corinth. The archaic temple (on the right).

CORINTH

The destruction of Corinth in 146 B.C. stands as a crucial demarcation line in the history of the city and its monuments. The ruins of the archaic temple on the low hill of the agora are the only visible traces of the pre-Roman city. The other important ruins in the area belong to the Roman imperial and Christian era.

The Greek Archaeological Service began to excavate Corinth in 1892. The results, however, were not very impressive, as excavations were not carried out near the temple, where the agora was, but in the surrounding area and near some sections of the long walls. Systematic excavation was begun in 1896 by the American School of Classical Studies in Athens, and has been continued with small interruptions to this day over the entire site of the ancient city.

Most of the ruins uncovered by the excavations belong to the Roman Imperial period, and to the city as rebuilt by Julius Caesar and Augustus. Very few remains survive from Greek times, because of the total destruction of the city in 146 B.C.

Amongst these few remains is the temple of Apollo, a Doric peripteral temple from the middle of the sixth century B.C. The spring to the south of this is contemporary with it, as is the original core of the springs of Peirene and Glauke. The meagre remains that are preserved of the ancient stadium, to the

The Roman Odeion of ancient Corinth. The Acrocorinth can be seen in the background.

south-east of Peirene, belong to the Classical period, as do the small temple in the centre of the west side of the precinct of Apollo, the north stoa, and the south stoa. The north-west stoa, to the south of the ancient temple, behind the Roman buildings, dates from the Hellenistic period.

During its reconstruction, the city acquired a Roman character in architectural as well as other respects. Those of the earlier monuments that escaped total destruction were repaired or converted in accordance with the demands of Roman architecture.

The archaic temple

Seven monolithic Doric columns from the west and north side-row of columns still remain standing. The temple was peripteral, with 6 columns on the narrow sides and 15 on the long sides. There were also two Doric columns between antae of the pronaos and the opisthodomos, and two inner rows of columns in the cella to support the roof. Chronologically the temple belongs to the decade after 550 B.C. (it was built after the fall of the Cypselids). An older temple is known to have existed on the same site during the tyrants' rule; it was built about a century earlier. When Corinth was rebuilt in Roman times, the temple was restored and dedicated to Apollo.

Plan of all the foundations excavated in the agora of Corinth. On the left are the theatre and the odeion, in the centre the archaic temple, and on the right, the Lechaion road.

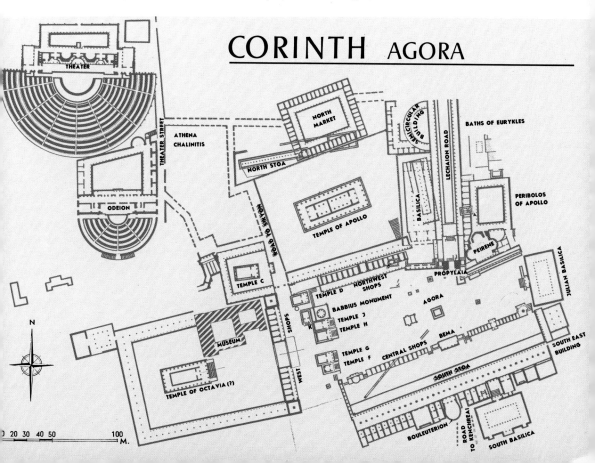

The seven monolithic Doric columns surviving from the peristyle of the archaic temple (of Apollo).

Reconstruction of the temples in the west wing of the agora. From the left: temple F, usually identified with that of Tyche; temple G, normally thought of as the Pantheon; temple H (possibly of Herakles); temple J (possibly of Poseidon); the monument of Babbius, a small peripteral building; temple D (perhaps of Hermes).

Structures in the agora - The west wing

A number of small temples belonging to Roman Corinth were built on the west side of the agora. This was the most suitable side for building temples, as their entrance had to face east. Chronologically, they belong to the Imperial period after the birth of Christ. The temples H and J are known to have been built after A.D. 160. As Roman buildings, they differ from the ordinary Greek temples: they stood on a podium, i.e. a rectangular pedestal or elevated platform, and several steps led into them from the east. It is not known to which gods they were dedicated. For the rest of the buildings the meagre indications resulting from the excavations, combined with Pausanias' description, have caused the following theory to prevail: temple D was dedicated to Hermes — Pausanias reports having seen a statue of Hermes in it, while another statue of the same god stood outside the shrine, perhaps on the round pedestal that stood very near the south side of the small cella. Temple K, which for reasons of space had its entrance on the south side, contrary to the rule, was of such small dimensions that it could only have served to house one of the celebrated statues of the agora (probably a statue of Clarian Apollo).

In front of temple D there is an open area that is thought by some to be a precinct dedicated to all the gods ("Pantheon"). This view necessitates renaming the buildings in the west of the agora, the order of which is reversed. Temple D should be ascribed to the goddess Tyche, temple G to Clarian Apollo and temple F to the goddess Aphrodite.

This must have also been the purpose of the small, round, adjacent peripteral structure. There was a Latin inscription on the architrave of this building, several fragments of which have survived; the inscription informs us that it was built by Gn. Babbius Philinus, a local *aedilis and pontifex,* also a benefactor of the Roman province of Corinth. He is known to us from two other inscriptions as dedicator to Poseidon. As he also bore the Greek name of Philinus, it appears he must have been a liberated slave of Greek origin; having come from Rome to Corinth, he became attached to the city and embellished it with various edifices, among which the elegant round marble structure in the agora, which consisted of an elevated square platform, upon which there was a circular row of eight Corinthian columns supporting an Ionic entablature with a conical marble roof.

The excavations have revealed that on the spot of the temples H and J, mentioned above, there existed in former times (at least until A.D. 160) an impressive fountain with a bronze statue of Poseidon. The statue stood in the middle of the west side of the whole fountain structure. Pausanias saw this statue just after the mid-2nd century A.D. At a lower level, there were three rectangular basins placed in tiers, each of which filled with the water overflowing from the one above it.

Temple G is believed to be the pantheon of Corinth mentioned by Pausanias. It was a custom in those times for cities to dedicate a temple or a shrine to all the gods, so as to please anonymous or "unknown" deities among them. The smallest temple F, the last in the row, is believed to have been dedicated to the goddess Tyche (Fortune); in late antiquity every city took care to build temples and erect statues to Tyche, for this goddess symbolized both the city and its prosperity.

This interpretation of the structures, with the exception of the Babbius monument, is far from certain. It has recently been suggested that the temples should be renamed in reverse order: temple D should be ascribed to the goddess Tyche, the free space flanking it on the east side should be seen as the shrine of "all the gods", temple G should belong to Clarian Apollo and temple F to the goddess Aphrodite (a piece of marble with the inscription *Veneri* was found on this site). The structure standing opposite with the apse in the middle probably sheltered the statue of Hermes — whereas the prevailing view until now was that it had been sheltered in temple D.

The north wing

The row of sixteen small buildings, fairly well preserved belonged to the late Imperial years. The central vaulted room was used as a church in Christian times. Under the foundations of the first rooms on the east side, one can still see the foundations of an apsidal structure dating back to the 6th century B.C. It must have had some connection with the "sacred spring" which was situated further south, in the central section of the agora, below ground level; in later years this spring was reached by means of a stone staircase. The triglyphs (three-grooved tablets) and metopes which have survived used to adorn the wall that formed the more prominent part of the spring.

East of this row of rooms there was the impressive façade of a Roman basilica. The basilica itself stood further north, along the west edge of the Lechaion road. The front part of the basilica, facing the centre of the agora, also had a top storey. Its entablature had the same number of supports as the cornice of the ground floor, but the four middle columns were replaced on the upper storey by four supernaturally large sculptures of barbarians, who supported the architrave on their shoulders. Further east still, at the beginning of the Lechaion road, there was an imposing gateway (*propylaia*) which was reconstructed several times in a different form. At one stage of its history, this gateway consisted of a large, central, arched entrance, flanked on either side by two lower entrances also arched. The central entrance was topped by gilt chariots ridden by Helios (the Sun) and his son Phaëthon.

Reconstruction of the monument dedicated by Babbius Philinus, a Roman of Greek descent who lived at Corinth. From the parts that have been preserved, it has been thought to have been a small circular peripteral building on a high square base, with 8 Corinthian columns and a round entablature, consisting of an architrave and decorative friezes of kymatia and anthemia. A Latin inscription on the architrave tells us that Babbius built it when he was Duovir of Corinth: GN(AIUS) BABBIUS PHILINUS, AED(ILIS) PONTIFEX D(E)S(UA) P(ECUNIA) F(ACIENDUM) C(URAVIT), IDEMQUE IIVIR (P(ROBAVIT).

Reconstruction of the north wing of the agora, with the commercial buildings and the two-storeyed façade of the basilica. The archaic temple, rebuilt in the Roman period, is in the

The central section of the agora

Part of the empty space at the centre of the agora during the years of Corinth's autonomy could also be used as the track of a stadium. The stone starting-line of the race-track can still be seen under the staircase leading into the Roman basilica; in Roman times a large statue of the goddess Athena stood in the middle of the agora. There was also an important altar for public sacrifices.

The basilica, which stood on the eastern edge of the central section of the agora, is believed to have been built by Augustus' family, who were also responsible for reconstructing the city; torsos of statues identified as representing Julius Caesar and Augustus were found in the basilica. It was mainly used as a court of justice and as a public meeting place.

A row of small shops or rooms stood along the south edge of the agora's central section, at the back of which the ground level is slightly higher. In the middle there was a kind of platform or tribune from which the Roman pro-consul addressed the citizens when they gathered in the central area. The Roman

background. On the right is the imposing propylon at which the Lechaion road ended. On top of the propylon are the bronze gilt statues of Helios and Phaethon.

official reached the tribune either by crossing the empty space at the back or through the central section and up the steps that led to the tribune. In A.D. 52, the Apostle Paul was brought to this spot in the presence of the pro-consul Lucius Julius Gallio, Seneca's brother (see Acts, 18, 12-17), to answer accusations by the Hebrews of Corinth, who found that his preaching undermined Mosaic Law and caused dissension between the Hebrews and Paul's supporters in Corinth. Gallio's verdict was that Paul's teachings did not constitute an offence under Roman Law, and therefore let the Apostle continue his mission in peace, a fact which certainly helped to bring about the early foundation of a Christian Church in Corinth. It was to commemorate this event that a small church with three apses was built on the site in the Middle Ages; a few remains of the church can still be seen today.

The southern structures of the agora

During the 4th century B.C., a stoa (porticus), 160 meters long, with 71

Doric columns along the front side, was built behind the tribune and the row of central shops; it was reconstructed at the time of Corinth's refoundation. The stoa also included an inner colonnade of 34 Ionic columns. Further in, there was a row of 33 rooms, all of which were two-storeyed and divided into two square sections. There was a well in the outer square section of each room, supplied with water from the Peirene spring; the water-pipe ran the whole length of the stoa, under the floor of the rooms' front square sections. Right behind the stoa, there was a row of public establishments and a large Roman basilica built on the same plan and probably serving the same purpose as the basilica on the eastern side of the agora.

The Lechaion road

A few steps led down from the gateway on the south side of the agora to the paved Lechaion road. On either side of it there were narrow pavements edged with gutters that collected the rainwater. A number of stoas ran parallel on either side of the road. Through one of these stoas, at the beginning of the east side of

The paved Lechaion road, with its footpaths, also paved, and gutters. The Acrocorinth can be seen in the background.

the road, one came to a series of shops. ore shops were to be found at the quadrilateral agora on the apposite (west) side of the road. A large semi-circular stoa was built over this agora at a later date.

The *Peirene fountain*, which was in itself an elaborate construction, was situated at a lower level and was reached by a number of steps. Its monumental aspect (it had three apses and walls faced with marble was the work of Herod Atticus in the 2nd century A.D. In its previous form, it had a central courtyard with six openings on its south side, through which one had access to an equal number of draw-basins. The basins were placed at a lower level than the court-yard, which meant that people who came for water had to go through the openings and descend a few steps to reach the basins.

The rectangular space with an inner peristyle directly north of the Peirene fountain was known as "the *precinct of Apollo*" and was probably used for open-air religious meetings. In pre-Roman years, there was also a small temple of Apollo on this site; its foundations have survived under the walls of the Roman shops mid-way along the west side of the precinct. North of the precinct, part of a structure used as a bath has been excavated. This is supposed to be the place

The ruins of the spring of Peirene, from the Roman imperial period. In the background are the 6 arched openings through which one went down to the bowls carved in the rock, to draw water.

where the baths of Eurycles were (known to us from literary sources). Eurycles was Augustus' contemporary.

The most important construction on the other side of the road was the large *Roman basilica;* its imposing façade, adorned with colossal figures of barbarians, looked out on the central section of the agora. To the north there was the old agora mentioned above and directly to the west, the new market. It was also quadrilateral, with an inner open-air space surrounded by a peristyle, as was the custom in Roman times for all agorae (market-places). This large edifice formed the north part of the archaic temple's precincts.

Other public buildings (theatre, odeon, temples and sanctuaries)

To the west of the archaic temple, at a relatively lower level, there are remains of the *theatre* of Corinth. The stage is the one that was in use in Roman times. On the same spot there are also vestiges of an earlier theatre (4th century B.C.). A theatre of the 5th century B.C., mentioned in ancient texts, was probably also situated there.

Slightly higher up south, one can see the remains of the cavea and the stage foundations of the Roman *odeon*.

The sanctuary of *Athena Chalinitis* (Bridling) is believed to have stood in the empty space directly to the east of the Odeon. The explanation for this attribute of the goddess can be found in ancient Corinthian myths, according to which Athena gave Bellerophon the celebrated bridle with which he was able to tame the winging horse Pegasus. It is possibly connected with the attribute *Hippia* (related to a horse) given elsewhere to the goddess Athena.

To the south, at a higher level still, there are remains of the *Glauce fountain*, hewn out of the rock and supplied with water by means of a water-pipe from the south. Continuing east, there is a temple with precinct which was possibly dedicated to *Hera Akraia*, whose cult was transferred from the Heraion of Perachora to Corinth. The temple was built at some time after the reconstruction of Corinth, in Roman times; but Hera's cult existed in the city during its period of autonomy.

Finally, there was a Roman peripteral temple standing on a high platform directly to the south-west of the modern museum. The temple is believed to have been dedicated to the patrician family who founded Roman Corinth, in other words, the gens Julia. This is probably the temple that Pausanias designated as *"the temple of Octavia"* (Augustus' sister), owing to the sculptured figure of Octavia, in the form of a Roman patrician lady seated upon a throne, which had been placed inside the temple as a symbol of the family.

Asclepieion - gymnasium

On the flat expanse about 400 meters north from the theatre, immediately within the north arm of the fortified enclosure of Corinth, archaeologists have

Reconstruction of Peirene in the Classical and Hellenistic periods (above) and the Roman imperial period (below).

Remains of the large peripteral temple attributed to Octavia. It had an enclosure with Corinthian columns. The temple was built on a podium surrounded by stoas.

excavated the Asclepieion of Corinth. This included a prostyle temple (with a portico of four columns in the front), in the middle of an enclosure which communicated on the west side with another square enclosure that consisted of an open space at the centre with colonnades on all sides. This second enclosure belonged to a fountain known as the Lerna.

At a small distance south of the Asclepieion (in the direction of the theatre) a long stylobate, as well as fragments of columns, have been visible at all times. This is where the gymnasium of Corinth is believed to have stood.

Reconstruction of the spring of Glauke. The bowls were approached by a staircase carved in the rock.

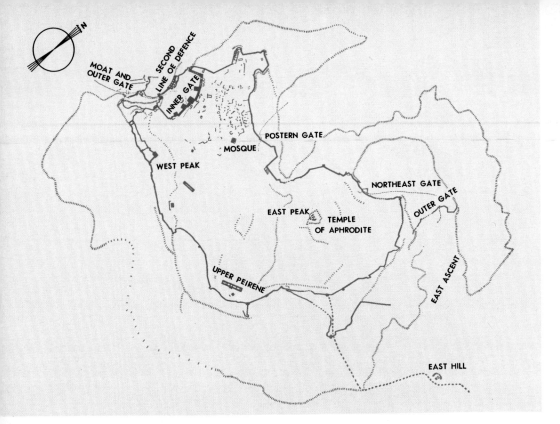

Plan of the walls on the Acrocorinth. Medieval fortifications were erected on the ancient foundations. Parts of the ancient walls, particular near the gates and towers, were used in the medieval fortification.

ACROCORINTH

The steep, rocky hill that was the acropolis of ancient and medieval Corinth is 575 meters high (its highest peak), and is only accessible on its western face, which is reached by a winding road that used to go past a multitude of obscure sanctuaries, much frequented throughout antiquity by ordinary people practicing a warm, usually mystic cult. (Sanctuaries of Demeter and Kore, the Moires, the Great Mother, Helios, Isis, Serapis.)

The hill was well fortified both in pre-Christian times and in the Middle Ages. The medieval fortifications are in many instances founded upon the ancient ones, or are simply a reconstruction and restoration of ancient walls and towers. On the west side, which is the only point of access, for greater safety there is a triple wall with three successive gates.

The famous temple of Aphrodite stood at the top of the hill; nothing has remained of it because other structures were built on the site (which is in a dominant position) in the Middle Ages and during the Turkish occupation. On the south side of the hill, near the top, but a little lower than the site of the temple, there is a spring, now reduced to a trickle below ground. As far back as late antiquity, the spring was reached by steps.

The series of gates leading up to the Acrocorinth, as rebuilt in the medieval period. In front of the outer gate there was a dry moat, and a bridge over this can be seen.

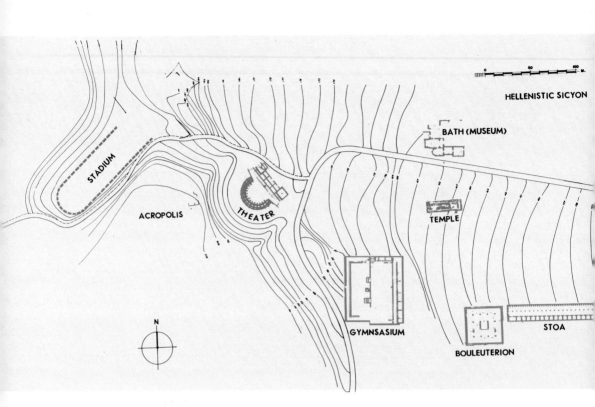

STADIUM

ACROPOLIS

THEATER

BATH (MUSEUM)

TEMPLE

GYMNSASIUM

BOULEUTERION

STOA

N

Plan of Hellenistic Sicyon. The theatre, gymnasium, bath and a long stoa are all marked.

SICYON

The "Sicyonian plain", as the fertile coastal plain that lies near Kiato and Velo was known in antiquity, used to belong to the ancient state of Sicyon. The treasure of Sicyon at Delphi is an indication of the prosperity of this city during the 5th century B.C. At Delphi we can also see another sign of Sicyon's former wealth, which left brilliant memories to the very end of antiquity: it was a round, monopteral structure that served to shelter an opulent bronze offering commemorating the victory of Cleisthenes at *Pythia* in 582 B.C.

In pre-Hellenistic times, Sicyon was built in the green, richly cultivated plain lying between Kiato and Vassiliko. However, Demetrios Poliorcetes, who had control of the region in 303 B.C., found the city was too vulnerable in that position, and had it moved higher up, to a position that had once been used as an acropolis, overlooking the bed of the river Asopos. Long before the move, in Archaic times, there, were already a number of sanctuaries and farmhouses on that vast tableland. Under Demetrios' guidance, the position was fortified, most of the required public buildings were erected, and the inhabitants of the old city were encouraged and assisted in settling on the new site. Demetrios tried to give the new city the name of Demetrias, but the Sicyonians soon reverted to its old name.

Pre-Roman Sicyon was famous for its important schools of sculpture, paint-

The Roman bath of Sicyon, recently restored and now used as a museum.

ing and bronze-work. The most famous shrines of Hellenistic Sicyon were those of *Akraia Tyche* and the Dioskouroi on the acropolis, and the temples of Dionysos, Athena, Asklepios, Aphrodite, Demeter, and Hera. There was also a council-house (bouleuterion) stoa and a gymnasium.

The agora of Hellenistic Sicyon

The village that now occupies the site of Hellenistic Sicyon was formerly known as Vassilika, and then as Vassiliko, and has now been renamed Sicyon. There is a public highway leading from Kiato to modern Sicyon. After crossing the village, the road reaches the ruins of Hellenistic Sicyon at a small distance to the west.

The most prominent structure is a *Roman bath*, made of flat baked bricks, as was the custom in late Roman times. After the excavations conducted by the Archaeological Service, it was restored and is now used as a museum. Opposite this structure, on the south side, there was the Hellenistic agora. The nearest remains that were excavated on this site are foundations of poros stone belonging to a very elongated temple (a little more than 38 m. long and 11.3 m. wide). As this elongated plane is characteristic of pre-classical temples and as the foundations, at least, are made of poros stone, it is believed the temple belongs to the Archaic period. There can be no doubt that the temple was reconstructed

One of the two springs of the gymnasium of Sicyon, after excavation and restoration.

at the time of the foundation of Hellenistic Sicyon.

Further south excavations revealed the foundations of a large square structure (40.5 × 41.15 m.) with 16 inner columns serving to support the roof. It is believed to have been used originally as a bouleuterion (council-house); the speaker's tribune was a square platform in the middle. In later years it was used as a bathing-establishment.

Directly east of this structure, a long *stoa* was excavated. It was 106 m. long and 6 m. wide, and had 47 here was also an inner colonnade consisting of 24 Ionic columns, behind which stood a row of 20 uniform rooms that were used as shops.

The gymnasium

On the uphill section lying west of the central part of the agora, excavations brought to light a large *gymnasium* which is believed to be the gymnasium mentioned in various literary sources as having been founded by Cleinias, Aratos' father. As it now stands, it consists of two flat rectangular sections at different levels. The upper section (70 × 32.5 m.), with stoas on all sides except for the west, is believed to be a later addition. In the middle of the west side, a staircase was discovered, leading to the lower rectangular section; this was more spacious than the upper section and was used as the gymnasium proper. Along this side there is a retaining wall supporting the upper section. In the middle of

The theatre of Sicyon. The lower seats of the koilon, the left parodos and the remains of the skene can be seen.

the wall, there is the staircase, and on either side of it a fountain with two front columns *in antae*. On the other three sides, there were also colonnades (with rooms at the back) opening into an inner central space.

The theatre and the stadium

At a short distance north-west of the gymnasium, excavations brought to light the *theatre* which is the second most important ruin of Sicyon after the Roman bath. Two stone vaulted passages have survived in fairly good condition on the north and south sides of the theatre cavea; they led directly from the slope of the hill to the upper tiers of the theatre. The foundations of the stage, the embankments retaining the side-entrances, the lower rows of seats and the semi-circular orchestra were also completely unearthed in the course of the excavations.

The site of the stadium is easily discernible owing to the conformation of the ground. It lies north-west of the theatre. A tall wall, polygonally built, has survived: it served as the embankment for the *sphendone*, the sling-shaped curve at one end of the stadium.

The top of the hill overlooking the theatre and stadium was used as the acropolis of Hellenistic Sicyon. In Roman times, literary sourses tell us, there were sanctuaries for the goddess Tyche (Fortune) and the Dioscuri on the hilltop.

TITANE

Titane was situated on the border between ancient Sicyon and Phleiasia; it was reached by a road that started from Sicyon and proceeded south, almost, parallel to the river Asopos. An easier approach nowadays is via Kiato, along the Soulion-Gonoussa-Titane highway. After Titane, the road slopes down into the plain of Nemea.

The modern village of Titane — formerly known as Voivoda — is at a small distance below the hill on which once stood the *acropolis* of ancient Titane. This hill is now topped by the small village cemetery and an old chapel, Saint Tryphon, into which a number of ancient stones have been incorporated. The ancient wall, made of ashlar blocks, has survived on three of the four sides of the hill; the east side is missing because the fortifications were interrupted at that point on account of the extreme abruptness of the slope, as opposed to the other sides, which are only slightly more prominent than the surrounding flat expanse. From the steep east side of the hill, one can see the bed of the river Asopos descending from Phleiasia and going out to sea at a short distance east of Kiato.

Ancient Titane was famous for its *Asclepieion*. A votive inscription to Asclepios is still incorporated in the south wall of the cemetery chapel, but it is believed that the sanctuary was situated on the even ground west of the hill, where there was an ancient settlement and where the foundations of a Roman bath have been recently excavated. Pausanias mentions the existence of a temple of Athena on the acropolis.

PHLIUS

The sovereignty of ancient Phlius or Phleius extended to the Phleiasian plain, which used to produce the "Phleiasian wine", famous in antiquity. It is now known as the plain of Nemea, which is also well-known for its wines.

The site of Phlius is about 3.5 kilometers north-west from modern Nemea (formerly known as Aghios Georghios). The modern highway connecting Nemea to Titane and ending up at Kiato just bypasses the ancient site. This highway goes past a small hill on the right (in the direction of a village called Koutsi) which was once the fortified *acropolis* of Phlius. No visible remains of the walls have survived.

The church of the Panayia on the west slope of the hill is believed to occupy the site of the ancient *Asclepieion* which is known to have existed at Phlius. The *agora* was near the slope where the *theatre* has been recently excavated. The lower rows of seats, made of poros stone, and part of the stage have recently been unearthed.

Directly south of the theatre, excavations have revealed the foundations of a large rectangular structure (which has been given the designation of "palace"), approximately 36 × 26 meters. On each side of this structure there was an inner colonnade of Doric columns (5 on the north and south sides, and 8 on the east and west sides — 22 columns in all). There was an open courtyard in the middle. This structure is believed to belong to the 5th century B.C.; it was destroyed in the Roman period and reconstructed in the 2nd century A.D., remaining in use until the 4th century A.D. at least. It served various purposes at various times; at one point it appears to have been used as an agora.

CLEONAE

Cleonae is one of those Greek cities that reached their peak in prehistoric times, survived in historical times as townships or obscure rural communities, and vanished completely before the end of the ancient world.

The plain of Cleonae, like that of Phlius further west, had an important city as its capital. We know that in prehistoric times there was an important settlement in the plain of Cleonae, on a small eminence near the modern railway-station of Aghios Vassilios (near at Zygouries). When this settlement fell into decline, Cleonae rose to prominence, at a short distance north. Homer uses the phrase "euktimenas Kleonas" (well-inhabited, well-built) for the fist or second of these settlements.

In historical times, the *acropolis* of Cleonae was on a small hill 4 or 5 kilometers south-east of the modern village of Kontostavlos, which is officially known as Ancient Cleonae. However, the acropolis and the city of Cleonae of historical times is nearer to the modern suburb of the Aghios Vassilios railway-station, from which a highway leads to Kontostavlos and then to Nemea. A country lane on the right of the highway, at a distance of 2 or 2.5 kms. from the Aghios Vassilios railway-station leads eastwards to the Heraklion, a small sanctuary situated outside the walls of Cleonae, and then to the ancient city itself. The hill of the acropolis had a special fortified enclosure and was situated on the northern edge of the fortified city. Only a few insignificant remains of both enclosures have survived. At the Heraklion, the foundations of the *temple* have been found in better condition; the temple consisted of a small cella, with an entrance on the east side consisting of a *prostoon* with four columns; at a short distance to the east, there was a walled enclosure with two altars that have been ascribed (not very convincingly) to the malignant Elian heroes, Eurytus and Cteatus, Heracles' enemies; according to tradition, Heracles killed both of them at Cleonae, as they were about to go to the Isthmus for the games. The floor of the *cella* is paved with well-trimmed blocks of stone. Part of the walls have also survived. The Cleoneans honoured Herakles for another local exploit as well; it is mentioned in Greek mythology that he slew the lion of Nemea at Mount Tretus, not far away.

The acropolis of Titane, with parts of the ancient walls and towers.

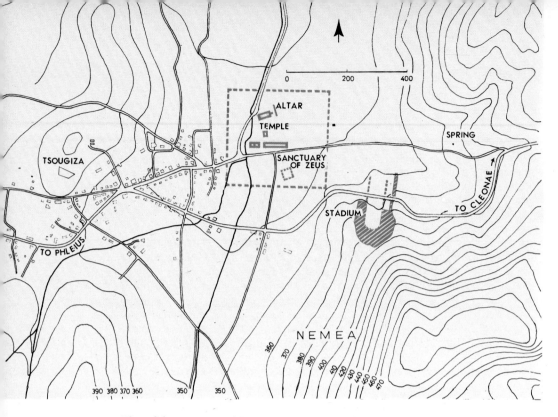

Plan of the sanctuary of Zeus at Nemea. The stadium is 500 m. south-west of the temple. Excavation of it has recently started.

NEMEA

The valley of Nemea is about 8.5 kms. south-east of Phlius, but it belonged to Cleonae (before the ascendancy of Argos); Cleonae was situated at a shorter distance to Nemea.

The meaning of the toponym is meadow, or pasture. This small, grassy valley sheltered a *sanctuary* dedicated to Zeus, worshipped together with the hero Opheltes, in honour of whom Panhellenic games were celebrated every two years. Opheltes was the son of the local king, Lycourgos. When the seven Argive generals reached Nemea in their march against Thebes, Opheltes was still only an infant. His nurse, Hypsipyle, put him down in the grass (among which grew clusters of wild celery) in order to show the generals the way to the spring; but a snake hidden in the grass bit the child and caused it to die. According to tradition the Nemean games were initiated by the seven chiefs in honour of the dead child, in the same spirit that the Isthmian games had been introduced in honour of the dead boy Palaimon. The award for the winners of the Nemean games was a crown of wild celery. Archaeological finds which may have some connection with the mythical age of Nemea come from the prehistoric settlement unearthed on the west fringes of the modern village of Nemea, on the eminence known as Tsoungiza. There exist remains from all the successive phases of the Bronze Age.

The most impressive monument of historical Nemea is the *temple of Zeus*. Three of its Doric columns have remained standing: one on the east wing of the peristyle and two in the pronaos, which used to stand between the antae. During the excavations, the groundwork of the temple and the *adyton* at the west

The three columns of the temple of Zeus at Nemea still standing. The two with the fragment of the architrave belong to the pronaos, and the other to the pteron.

extremity of the secos, in place of the opisthodomos, were completely cleared of covering layers of soil. The adyton is a well-built structure about two meters deep under the floor of the *cella*, and can be reached by some steps hewn into the rock. It is 4 m. long and a little more than 3.5 m. wide. It was made of stone blocks similar to the ones used for the platform of the temple, and belongs to the same period (330-320 B.C.). This was also the site of an earlier temple belonging to the Archaic period. The pit-like hollow was probably used for the cult of the hero Opheltes, or Archemoros as he was also known. The surviving temple was peripteral, with 6 × 12 Doric columns and a stylobate 42.55 × 22 meters. On the east side of the temple one can see remains of the foundations of a long and narrow altar, which has been cleaned recently.

At about 75 meters south of the temple's platform there are some remains of the foundations of a large structure (approximately 86 × 20 meters) that was probably used as a guest-house; on the top of these, one can see the ruins of a Christian church. Between the temple and the guest-house there are the remains of another structure which has been identified as a stoa or as the precinct of a place of worship; west of the guest-house, there are the ruins of a palaistra with an adjacent bath. The west section of these ruins has been repaired.

The *stadium* of Nemea, which is now being excavated, is about 500 meters east of the sanctuary on the slope of the hill, and to the right of the highway to Kontostavlos. The excavations have brought to light the stone starting-point of the race-track and at about 180 meters opposite, the embankment retaining the race-track. This distance allows us to assume that the length of the "stadion" run in the Nemean races was shorter than the Olympian, Panathenean and even the Isthmian stadia.

MUSEUMS AND ARCHAEOLOGICAL COLLECTIONS
OF CORINTHIA

THE MUSEUM OF CORINTH

Finds from the Corinthian excavations are housed in the museum which was built in the north-west corner of the archaeological site of ancient Corinth by a donation of Ada Small Moore of the American School of Classical Studies.

On the wall facing the entrance hangs a floor mosaic with a representation of griffins from the 4th century B.C.

The finds are displayed in four rooms and in porticoes around the central courtyard, enabling the visitor to become familiar with the evolution of culture in Corinthia over the centuries.

In the *first room,* at the left of the entrance, are cases displaying finds from prehistoric excavations such as vases from the Neolithic, Early, Middle and Late Helladic through the Mycenaean periods, figurines, utensils (whetstones and stone axes), carved steatite, obsidian blades, pieces of jewelery (stone needles, glass beads and necklace beads), some small fragments of frescoes and one Early Cycladic figurine.

The second room on the right of the entrance contains noteworthy finds of the Archaic through the Classical periods. On the left as one enters, there is a sarcophagus showing the burial of a youth. In the cases are displayed vases of the Protogeometric, Geometric, Protocorinthian and Corinthian periods with representations which show an Oriental influence. There are also Attic red-figured and black-figured vases, small altars found in houses and tombs of the 6th to the 2nd centuries B.C., clay models of chariots and of an oven, clay figurines and lamps.

Pieces of special interest are: a relief synthesis of the Archaic period showing the Amazonomachy at the far end of the room; the head of a youth from the late Archaic period and some fragments of clay sphinxes of the Archaic period which have kept their original colors. Colors are also very well preserved on the wings of a slightly larger headless sphinx. Other interesting exhibits are a copper mirror with a representation of a woman with her hairdresser and slave, and several inscribed clay tablets of the 8th century B.C. bearing some of the first known examples of the Greek alphabet. On the top of the cases are placed amphorae and kraters.

The sculptures found in the excavations have all been collected in the *third room*. These consist of statues of Roman rulers, especially members of the Julia family who where honored as the "builders" of Corinth, and some busts and fragments of reliefs, also from Roman times. There are as well two larger than

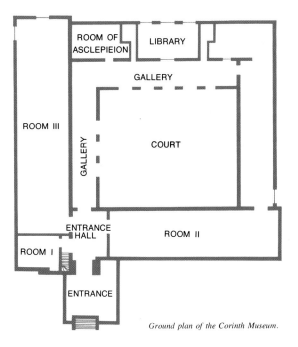

ROOM OF ASCLEPIEION

LIBRARY

GALLERY

ROOM III

GALLERY

COURT

ENTRANCE HALL

ROOM II

ROOM I

ENTRANCE

Ground plan of the Corinth Museum.

life statues of barbarian slaves which supported the root of a two storey stoa in the agora, a Roman copy of the head of Doryphoros from the original by Polykleitos, and a sarcophagus with decorations in relief representing the expedition of the Seven against Thebes. In the same room are floor mosaics from Roman buildings, and Roman frescoes. A rich collection of Byzantine pottery is in the cases. There are several articles of art, made of bronze, glass and ivory.

The *fourth room* (the room of the Asclepieion) contains finds from the Asclepieion of Corinth: metopes, fragments of statues, votive offerings and inscriptions. In the cases are weapons and jewelery from the time of the Turkish occupation.

In the porticoes around the central courtyard are displayed stone reliefs depicting the Amazonomachy, Gigantomachy and the labors of Herakles. There is also a sarcophagus of the 6th century B.C. and some inscriptions, among them one referring to the construction of the transisthmian wall by Justinian and his architect, Victorinus.

THE MUSEUM OF ISTHMIA

The collection is housed in a new building next to the archaeological site. It contains finds from excavations at Isthmia and Cenchreai such as pottery and pieces of minor arts of all periods, marble sculpture and Roman mosaics. The collection (not yet open to the public) is continually enriched with new discoveries.

Amongst the finds worth noting are the small gold Daric staters, the collection of lamps, and the pieces of ivory that were used to decorate chests.

Amongst these last the two small plaques with depictions of philosophers are of particular interest. There are also dedicatory panathenaic amphoras, athletic equipment (jumping weights) and two perirrhanteria. One of them is supported by an alternating sequence of korai and goats' heads; this is the archaic perirrhanterion discovered in the sanctuary of Poseidon.

The chief interest of the collection lies in the mosaics of glass panels which were recovered from Cenchreai. They were found in pairs, face to face in crates, and this led the excavators to the conclusion that they had not been used. The earthquake that struck the area resulted in their being washed into the sea, most of them being totally destroyed. The panels are of foreign make — probably Egyptian — and were apparently intended to be used to decorate the walls. They are made of coloured glass and a kind of plaster, in a technique called *opus sectile*. They have a variety of motifs: plants, decorative patterns, birds, and human figures, amongst which the depictions of Plato and Homer are particularly interesting. The pictures of the buildings by the sea and harbour installations are also impressive. The visitor gets a better impression of the colours and motifs with the aid of the reconstructions in colour on display in the cases next to the exhibits.

THE MUSEUM OF SICYON

A local museum became necessary after Prof. A. Orlandos' extensive excavations near Vassiliko in order to house archaeological finds from Hellenistic Sicyon, as well as finds from the older city in the plain. For this purpose Prof. Orlandos repaired part of the Roman bath where the walls were still standing to a considerable height and constructed a roof over three large rooms. Today these contain collected inscriptions and sculptures, some from the Archaic period and many from Hellenistic and Roman times. Pottery found in the excavations and numerous isolated finds from the *lower* city are also exhibited there. Vases and figurines from all periods are displayed along with some Mycenaean vases from the vicinity of Xylokastro. Floor mosaics from houses of the Hellenistic period with themes and representations of griffins have been placed on the walls. The mosaic work in black and white pebbles is worth noticing.

A bronze mirror with the handle fashioned into a woman was found in a woman's grave in older Sicyon. Striking among the sculptures is a head in Praxitelian technique.

Sculptures of the early Christian and Byzantine periods may be seen in the courtyard.

THE NEMEA MUSEUM

Since 1974 the University of California at Berkeley, under the auspices of the American School of Classical Studies and the supervision of the Archaeological Service of the Ministry of Culture, has been conducting large-scale excavations at Nemea.

The finds from these investigations are housed in the Nemea Archaeological Museum, built thanks to a generous gift from Rudolph A. Peterson and several other private citizens, which was inaugurated in 1984. Exhibits include finds from the valley of Ancient Nemea, as well as from the valleys of Cleonae and Phlius.

Incorporated in the museum lobby are commemorative plaques bearing the names of Rudolph A. Peterson and the other donors, as well as those of the workmen and local people who gave of their time and toil to the Nemea excavations between 1973 and 1983. Displayed in the middle of the hall are views of Nemea, captured for posterity by earlier travellers from 1766 onwards.

Housed in the central gallery are finds from the Sanctuary of Zeus and the Stadium of Nemea, the prehistoric settlement on Tsoungiza hill, the Mycenaean settlement at Aghia Irene and from the Mycenaean cemetery at Aidonia. The large windows of the gallery, which offer a vista of the Sanctuary of Zeus, and the large model of this (made by Robert Garbisch), enable the visitor to associate the objects in the museum with the corresponding sectors of the sanctuary and thus acquire an overall picture of Nemea and the area in which the games were held.

A large wall map to the left of the entrance and the cases containing silver and bronze coins from numerous Greek cities indicate the regions of the ancient world from which visitors came to Nemea (cases 1-3). Also exhibited are objects relating to the mythological traditions of Nemea and cult practices connected with the worship of the hero Opheltes (cases 4-6). To the right of the model of the sanctuary is one of the stadium. The objects displayed to the right of that are connected with the stadium and athletic activities at Nemea: stones from the starting line of the stadium, clay water conduits of the Roman period, statue bases and bronze strigils, javelin tips, a lead dumbbell and part of a stone one, an iron discus, iron spits, vases, fragments of bronze statues and a bronze plaque with votive inscription, which was attached to a statue of a horse dedicated to Zeus (case 7).

The finds in the centre of the gallery were discovered in wells and reveal many interesting details of the history of Nemea (cases 8, 9, 18). This information is complemented by architectural members from the original temple of Zeus, tools, materials and equipment from the workshops of a bronze founder and a carver of Pentelic marble (the stone used for the sima of the fourth-century BC temple of Zeus), as well as a model of the system of sloping roofs applied to the temple of Zeus (cases 19, 20).

The east end of the gallery is devoted to prehistoric finds: vases, figurines, tools and weapons covering the Early Neolithic to the Late Helladic period, mainly coming from the eminence of Tsoungiza (cases 12, 13).

There is an abundance of finds from the rich cemetery at Aidonia and the Mycenaean settlement at Aghia Irene: vases, figurines, gold finger rings, necklaces of glass paste beads or of gold, gold rosettes, sealstones, imitation scarabs, ivory rosettes, spindle whorls, a bronze dagger and arrow heads (case 14-17).

Displayed in the atrium are architectural members, sculptures and inscriptions from the fourth-century BC temple of Zeus, House 9 and other buildings at Nemea, as well as from other regions in the vicinity, such as Phlius and Petri.

Corinth Museum

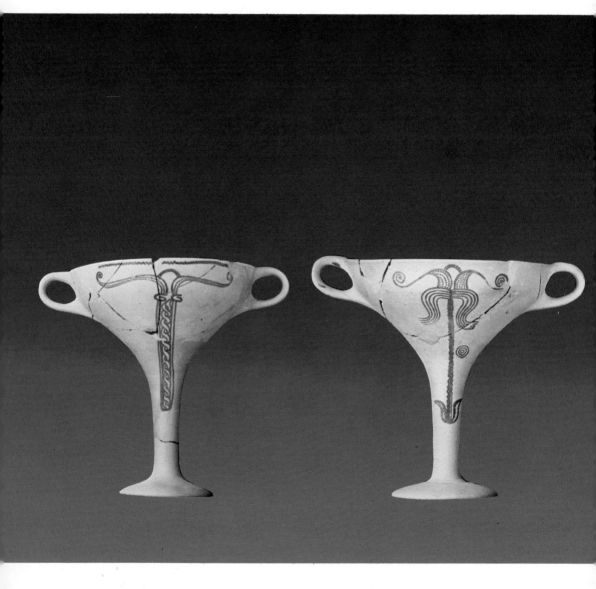

1. *Mycenaean kylikes. 13th century B.C.*
2. *Geometric oinochoe on a three-footed base. 8th century B.C.*
3. *Corinthian olpe, unique among the finds at Corinth. Upper band with animal frieze (hound, hare and goat). Reddish — brown glaze. 6th century B.C.*

3

4. *Corinthian oinochoe with figured decoration. ca. 600 B.C.*
5. *Corinthian alabastron; animal frieze with an owl at the center. ca. 600 B.C.*
6. *Corinthian figured aryballos. Two cocks facing, left right; in the middle small swan with closed wings. 625-600 B.C.*
7. *Corinthian figured skyphos, in frieze a Siren facing left, head turned back, wings spread. 625-600 B.C.*
8. *Figured amphora with lid. Cocks comb to comb over a double palmette design. ca. 600 B.C.*

9. *Excellent Corinthian aryballos with frieze of seven warriors. The artist was trying to depict an heroic action. 7th century B.C.*

10. *Corinthian aryballos. The young Pyrvias is leading a dancing chorus. ca. 600 B.C.*

11. *Interior of an attic black-figured kylix. Sphinx. Second half of 6th century B.C.*

12. *Attic black-figured kylix depicting a charioteer driving a quadriga with two sphinxes. Second half of the 6th century B.C.*

13-14. Green glazed "modiolus" from Cenchreai. The relief decoration combined the techniques of barbotine and appliqué ornamentation. Leaves, tendrils and fruit of the

grape, ivy and olive. On the front two birds. The vessel was probably made in Asia Minor during the early 1st century A.D.

15. *Mosaic from the Roman villa. A herder playing a flute with the herd pasturing nearby.*

16. *Mosaic from the Roman villa. Head of Dionysus framed by ornaments.*

18

17. Head of Aphrodite. ca. 300 B.C.
18. The right end of the sarcophagus (fig. 19) representing the death of Opheltes or Achemorus, which occured during the sojourn of the Seven at Nemea. 2nd century A.D.
19. Sarcophagus representing the departure of the Seven against Thebes. 2nd century A.D.

20. *Head of Dionysus from the Roman period.*

21. Roman head of the goddess Tyche. 1st century A.D.

22

23

22, 25. *Two collosal statues from the "captives façade".*
23. *Charming female head from the period of Hadrian, 2nd century A.D.*

24

24. *Head of Nero, son of Germanicus. The light beard on the cheeks and below the chin is doubtless a sign of mourning. 1st century A.D.*

26. *Male figure from a rectangular base. It represents Zeus Chthonios; he holds a cornucopia in his left hand and a phiale in his right, attributes of chthonic power. 1st century A.D.*

27. *Female figure (from the same rectangular base as figure 26) representing Demeter carrying wheat poppy-pods.*

28. *Armed statue from the Roman period. Over the tunic the figure wears an elaborate cuirass. 2nd century B.C.*

29. *Roman statue of Lucius Caesar (?). 1st century A.D.*

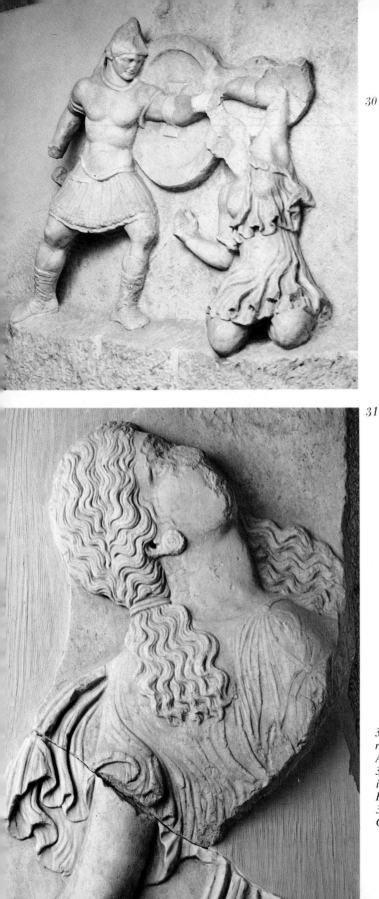

30

31

30. *Relief plaque from the Roman period representing a mythological scene; Amazonomachy.*

31. *Fragment of a marble relief preserving the upper part of a dancing maenad. Roman period. 2nd century A.D.*

32. *Relief plaque from the Roman period; Gigantomachy.*

Isthmia Museum

33. *Panel of opus sectile. Harbour structure. At the left two towers topped by a domical roof; Watchtowers or lighthouses (?). From Cenchreai.*
34. *Panel of opus sectile depicting the philosopher Plato(?). From Cenchreai.*

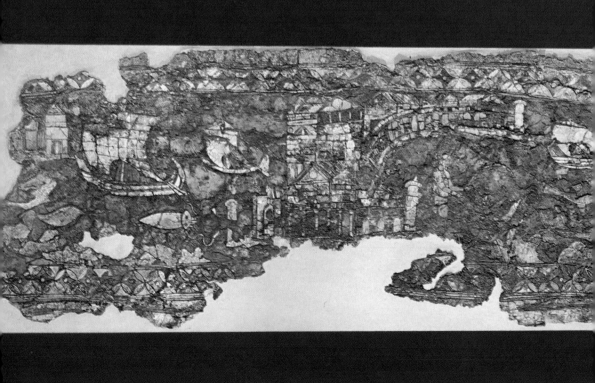

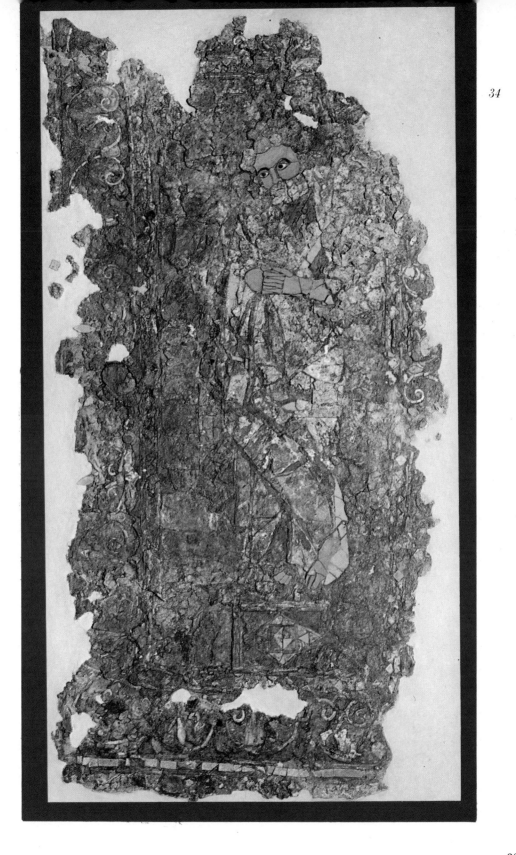

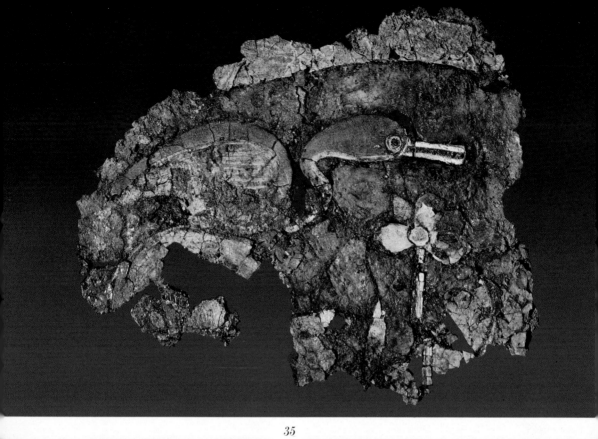

35

35. *Panel of opus sectile. Birds. Two of them rather like ducks. The other one is probably a flamingo. From Cenchreai.*
36. *Buildings along the harbour on a panel of opus sectile. The first building at the left end has a temple-like structure. From Cenchreai.*
37. *Reconstruction of the buildings depicted on the panel in figure 36.*

36

37

38-39. Two ivory plaques depicting seated men. Philosophers(?). From Cenchreai.

40. Marble head of a young athlete from Isthmia. Good Roman work

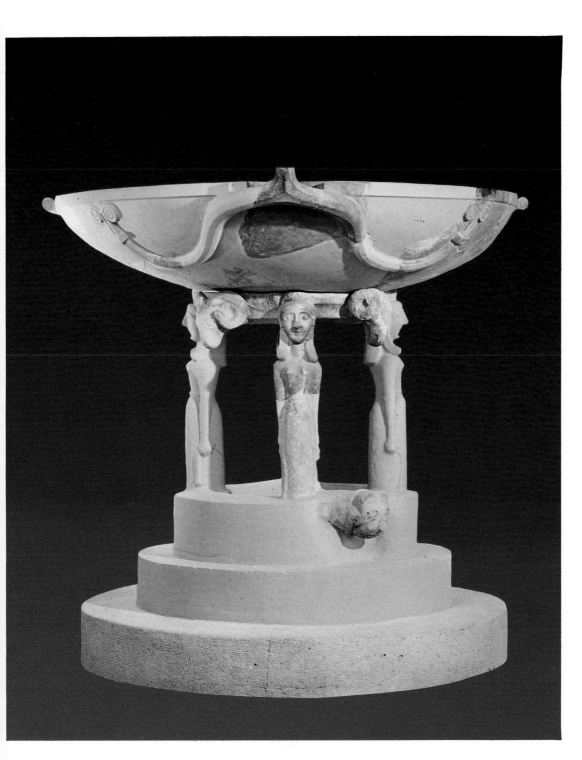

41. Archaic perirrhanterium from the sanctuary of Poseidon at Isthmia. 7th century B.C.

Sicyon Museum

42. *Statue of Artemis from the Roman bath at Sicyon. She is walking towards the left wearing boots. There is a hunting hound at her feet.*

43. *Marble statue of goat-footed Pan. He is wearing ox-skin. In his left hand he is holding a syrinx (Pan-pipe). A small goat can been seen at his feet. 2nd century A.D.*

44. *Statue of triple Hecate from the Roman bath at Sicyon. All three figures have a polos on their heads. One of them is holding a torch.*

42

43

14

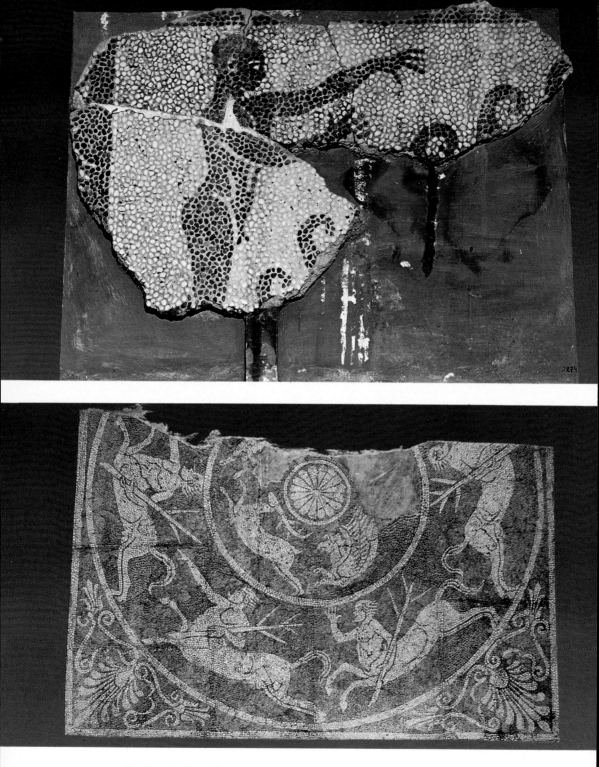

45. *Mosaic floor depicting a naked Aethiopian, stretching his hands before him. 4th century B.C.*

46. *Mosaic floor from a house at ancient Sicyon. Within a broad circular zone are preserved four centaurs (there were originally six) running one behind the other. Each is holding a large branch in his left hand. In the area within the zone of centaurs, are scenes*

47

48

of animals chasing each other. 4th century B.C.

47. *Fragment of a mosaic floor with the picture of a griffin.*
48. *Mosaic floor with a scene of animals running; a horse and a deer. Circular tessera; white and dark blue (almost black). 4th century B.C.*

BIBLIOGRAPHY

THE HERAION OF PERACHORA

The report on the Heraion excavations appeared in a edition in two volumes in 1940 and 1962, after the death of H. Payne, who directed the excavations. It was published by T.Y. Dunbabin and other collaborators of Payne, under the title *Perachora, The Sanctuaries of Hera Akraia and Limenia. Excavations of the British School of Archaeology at Athens in the Years 1930-1933.* This publication is supplemented by a very thorough study published by Humphrey Payne in 1931 on the subject of early Corinthian art, under the title *Necrocorinthia, A Study of Corinthian Art in the Archaic Period.* More recent works include J. Salmon's The Heraeum at Perachora and Early Corinth and Megara, *British School Annual* 1972, pp. 159-204, listing all studies posterior to 1933.

THE DIOLKOS

A basic work on this subject is N. Verdelis' Der Diolkos am Isthmus von Korinth, *Athenische Mitteilungen des Deutschen Archäologischen Instituts* 1956, p. 57 and following.

THE CANAL

Ps. Lucian's *Nero,* or *On the Opening of the Isthmus.* A detailed study of vestiges from the ancient project was made by a technician who took part in the opening of the modern canal: Bela Gerster (agent supérieur du Canal de Corinthe), L'Isthme de Corinthe, Tentatives de percement dans l'Antiquité, *Bulletin de Correspondance Hellénique* 1884, p. 225 and following.

THE SANCTUARY OF ISTHMIA

The definitive edition of the report on recent excavations at Isthmia carried out by the University of Chicago and the American School of Classical Studies in Athens, has now been complemented by Oscar Broneer, who was in charge of the excavations, in two volumes: *Isthmia, Temple of Poseidon* (1971), and *Isthmia, Topography and Architecture* (1973). A brief study on the theatre at Isthmia has also been published: *The Theatre at Isthmia* (1973), by Elisabeth Gebhard.

CENCHREAE

Reports on the Cenchreae excavations have been published by R. Scranton and E. Ramage in *Hesperia* 1964, p. 134 f. and 1967, pp. 124-186 and by Leila Ibrahim, Robert Scranton and Robert Brill in a volume : *Kenchreai, Eastern port of Corinth* (1976). There is a report on the basilica of Lechaion by D. Pallas in the Archaeological Deltion 1961-1962, Chron. 69 f.

Ancient Corinth

AGORA

Reconstruction

ACKNOWLEDGEMENTS

The publishers of this book are deeply indebted to the American School of Classical Studies for their courtesy in permitting the publication of plans and drawings, prepared by Dr. J. Travlos, Professor W.B. Dinsmoor Jr., Professor O.Broneer, P. de Jong and others, of the restored monuments of Ancient Corinth. The reconstruction of the buildings of the Corinthian agora and the topographic plan of Sicyon are from *Pausanias' description of Greece—Corinthiaka-Laconika,* by N.Papahatzis. The publishers also wish to thank Professor An. Orlandos for permission to publish for the first time his finds from Sicyon, Professor R.Scranton for permission to photograph and publish certain objects from the Isthmia Museum, Professor P.Clement for permission to publish for the first time the pictures of the mosaic floor from the Roman bath at Isthmia and Professor R.V. Schoder S.J. for permission to publish the air views of Heraion of Perachora, Isthmia, Cenchreai and Lechaion.

Coloured reconstructions of the monuments of Isthmia, Cenchreai and Ancient Corinth were prepared by the painter Stam. Vassiliou.

CORINTH

The definitive publication of the results of American excavations began in 1929, with the appearance of the first volume of the series, under the general title: *Corinth, Results of Excavations conducted by the American School of Classical Studies at Athens.* In the 25 odd volumes which have already been published, there are studies on the agora structures, the topography of Corinthia, Greek and Latin inscriptions, the theatre, the odeon, Acrocorinth, the Asclepieion, the fortifications of both Corinth and Acrocorinth, ceramics and sculptures of all the periods of Corinthian history and finally on the medieval buildings in the agora.

SICYON

Reports on the first American excavations of Sicyon have been published in the *American Journal of Archaeology* 1889, 1891, 1893, and 1934. Reports on the excavations conducted by the Greek Archaeological Society (A. Orlandos) appear in the Society's Practica (Practica Archaeologikis Etaireias) for the years 1933- 1954. A paper on the subject was published prior to the more recent excavations: Ch. Skalet, *Ancient Sicyon with a Prosopographia Sicyonia,* 1928. As regards the theatre, a relatively recent study (on the stage and orchestra) was published by E. Fiechter: *Antike Griechische Theaterbauten,* Heft 3: *Das Theater in Sicyon,* 1931.

TITANE

Titane has not yet been excavated. Ernst Meyer has published a topographical study on this site in *Peloponnesische Wanderungen,* 1939, accompanied by a plan of the acropolis and walls.

PHLIUS

A report on early American excavations at Phlius was published in *Art and Archaeology,* 1925, p. 23 and following. For more recent excavations, see *Hesperia* 1969, p. 443 f., 1971, p. 424 f., 1973, p. 102 f., 1975, p. 51 f.

NEMEA

C.W. Blegen has written about the prehistoric settlement south of Cleonae in his book entitled: *Zygouries, A Prehistoric Settlement in the valley of Cleonae,* 1928. A brief report on the excavation at the sanctuary of Heracles was published by Frickenhaus in *Archäologischer Anzeiger* 1913, p. 114 f. For prehistorical Nemea, see J. P. Harland's The Excavations of Tsoungiza, the prehistoric site of Nemea, *American Journal of Archaeology* 1928, p. 63 f. For the temple of Zeus, see R. Vallois' Le Temple de Zeus à Nemée, *Bulletin de Correspondance Hellénique* 1925, p. 1 f., and B.H. Hill's The Temple of Zeus at Nemea, 1966. Reports on earlier excavations: *American Journal of Archaeology* 1927, p. 421 f. Reports on recent excavations: C.K. Williams, *Archaeologicon Deltion* 1965, *Chronicle,* p. 154 f. For inscriptions, see *Hesperia* 1966, p. 320 f., and 1968, p. 381 f.